THE PATHWAY
TO POWERFUL

LEARNING TO LEAD A COURAGEOUS, CONNECTED CULTURE

CARLA CHUD
WITH DANNY SILK

TABLE OF

CONTENTS

1 | WE HAVE A PROBLEM!   5

2 | CONFRONTING POWERLESSNESS   21

3 | HEALING BROKEN PLACES   37

4 | BECOMING A POWERFUL LEADER   51

5 | INSTALLING A LENS OF HONOR   73

6 | EXCHANGING THE TRUTH   91

7 | CULTIVATING HEALTHY CONFRONTATION   107

8 | PROTECTING A POWERFUL CULTURE   123

Epilogue | BUILDING MOMENTUM IN A CULTURE OF HONOR   139

ACKNOWLEDGMENTS   143

1

WE HAVE A PROBLEM!

On a winter's day in 2013, I walked into our senior pastor's office with some bad news.

"Dennis, we are in serious financial trouble," I told him. "If the church continues to spend money at its current rate, I predict we will completely run out of money and be forced to close our doors within six months. The clock is ticking."

I had only been on staff for a couple months, filling the newly created position of finance manager. Until hiring me, the church had a bookkeeper who processed and deposited income, paid bills, and did payroll, but did not run or read financial reports. It had been a long time since anyone had taken a clear measurement of where the church stood financially. Having an accounting background, I immediately started to run reports, compare them to the budget, and assess the financial state of the organization. It didn't take me long to see that the numbers did not look good. The church had been shrinking in size for several years and income had decreased along with it. However, rather than noticing and addressing this problem, the leaders had continued to create budgets "in faith" that allowed the church to continue to spend at levels it couldn't afford, while praying for a miraculous turnaround. As a result, we had been losing money at an ever-increasing rate, and were now at the point where bankruptcy was imminent if nothing changed.

Dennis looked at me in total shock, clearly completely blindsided by this news. Finally, he asked, "What are we going to do?"

"I can't tell you, but you are going to have to do something. We absolutely cannot continue as we have been." I hesitated, then decided to point out an obvious but uncomfortable fact. "As it currently stands, our largest expense is staff. If you look at current church staffing practices, you will see that we are very overstaffed for a church our size."

I watched the weight of these words hit him. Dennis loved people, and the suggestion that he may have to let some staff members go, many of whom had worked at the church for a long period of time and felt like family to him, was especially painful. I left his office very doubtful that he would have the strength to make such a difficult leadership decision, even though I knew it was the only way that the church could be saved.

SYMPTOMS OF A DEEPER PROBLEM

When I had taken the position of finance manager, I was well aware that there were problems within the church, specifically among the leaders. My husband Aaron and I had been on staff previously for five years as youth pastors before stepping down in 2010, weary and beat-up after many experiences of dysfunctional communication and poor decision-making with the leadership team, and feeling powerless to fix these dynamics in the leadership culture. Upon returning to the church in 2012, we learned that the church had continued to struggle through major leadership changes, and that the unresolved conflict and division among the leaders and congregation had recently resulted in an unhealthy church plant. We had only agreed to me going back on staff because we thought the finance manager role would keep me mostly removed from those struggles. Instead, the finances had landed me squarely in the middle of broken leadership dynamics.

Before going to Dennis, I had brought the financial reports and analysis to my direct boss, a member of the senior leadership team. I explained the extent of the crisis and what would happen if we did nothing. He listened intently, asked questions, and took notes. However, when I returned a few weeks later to inquire what course of action we were going to take, I discovered he hadn't made any decisions about the information or passed it on to anyone. It was as if he had completely frozen in fear. It was after the third meeting where I heard he still hadn't acted that I took the news to Dennis myself, aware that we were losing time.

In contrast to my boss, Dennis didn't waste much time before bringing the news of the crisis to the entire senior team. However, it was then that the real weight of the disconnection that still existed among the leaders, three years on from when Aaron and I had left, became real to me. Here we were on the verge of losing everything, yet weeks turned into months as the team struggled to come together and build a solution to the problem. They seemed unwilling to look for the deeper issues driving the church's decline, instead proposing superficial changes while believing for a miraculous breakthrough. It was clear that the finances were only a symptom of the far deeper issues in our relational and leadership culture, which were now being forced into the open.

A TEAM DIVIDED

How did we end up in this state of crisis?

The church was now twenty years old. In its early years, it had grown and thrived, becoming one of the larger churches in the area. We attracted many families who built friendships, championed one another, spent time in and out of one another's homes, and experienced and grew in God together. We developed a reputation in our small area for being seeker-friendly and loving well, two factors that had contributed to rapid growth.

Yet even as we had grown, certain events in those early years had planted seeds of disconnection and mistrust among the core leadership team, which were never fully confronted and dealt with. The true impact of this oversight was revealed when, as is normal in the life cycle of all organizations, we came face to face with a series of challenges and conflict-producing events.

We went through a season of major change in vision and focus as a church when we got swept into the charismatic renewal/revival stream through exposure to Heidi Baker and Bethel Church in Redding, California. Our church had originally kept to a more conservative position—while we believed in the possibility of prophecy, miracles, and speaking in tongues, we did not actively pursue them as a congregation. As we embraced renewal, we began bringing in guest speakers and hosting conferences where miracles, signs, and wonders were on display. Some in the church were excited by this dramatic shift, while others were merely curious and still others were openly resistant, many leaving the church in quick succession. While the fresh move of God we were experiencing attracted a good number of people to the church, the loss of families that had been part of the church, some from the very beginning, was very painful and put an immense amount of pressure on the leaders. Some wanted to push forward and pursue the path we had chosen no matter the cost, while others wanted to slow down and find a balance that would preserve peace in our established congregation.

Managing the shift in our focus and expression was not the only problem facing the leadership in this season, however. Administrative weakness started to come to light, exposing the fact the church was failing financially. This put a large amount of strain on the elder board and pastors. At the time, we were an elder-led church, but there was confusion around responsibility and accountability between the elders and pastoral team. In response to the financial issues, the elders chose to get much more involved in the decisions of the church while remaining removed from its day-to-day operations, which ended up created frustration among those trying to implement those decisions. We also embarked on a very ambitious building project and fundraising campaign that not everyone was on board with, which drew another sharp line of division across our church. More families left, and the pain deepened for those who remained.

The stress of these problems created a situation where the church, which had felt like family to many, was now being torn apart. Division deepened as people began to assign blame to different parties—the senior pastor, associate pastors, or the elder board—for what was happening. Watching the leaders struggle to come together and pull in the same direction communicated to the staff and congregation a lack of clarity about what our vision truly was or who was leading. A leadership vacuum was established when no one stood up, said, "We have a problem," and pushed to bring the conflict to successful resolution.

The ability of any organization to successfully navigate a major change in direction is directly tied to the amount of trust that exists in the team leading the change. In fact, the success of any team's ability to achieve its goals is fundamentally built on trust. Trust is built in a team when, beginning with the leader, team members become unafraid of acknowledging the truth about themselves—their strengths and victories as well as their fears, struggles, and mistakes. A healthy culture of trust is built through the courageous, vulnerable, and safe exchange of truth. Only when the truth comes to light can differences be understood and confronted in a way that lowers fear, strengthens connection, and invites teammates to resolve problems together. Team members who trust one another with the truth will also champion one another in the process of development rather than withdrawing from one another when weakness is revealed, which strengthens the connection of the team. In an environment free of fear, creativity flourishes, ideas flow, problems are identified and resolved, and every person gets to contribute to the success of the organization—yielding strong results.

However, trust in a team gets undermined when people hide from the truth. When the leader refuses to confront their own fears and weaknesses, they will usually struggle with and mishandle weakness and mistakes in others. They will either passively avoid confronting problems that are affecting the connection or productivity of the team, or they will react harshly in punishment, sending the message that is it not safe to make a mistake and causing people to hide. When leaders take the path of avoidance or aggression and leave problems unresolved, fear begins to multiply in the silence, creativity is stifled, and the team loses its ability to be effective in working together to achieve its goals.

On our church's leadership team, the trust required to embark on new projects and navigate such major change simply didn't exist. When conflict arose, the team did not have the relational tools necessary to communicate honestly, seek understanding, and bring the conflict to successful resolution. We did not know how to confront our own fears and the differences between us by stepping into the vulnerable exchange of truth. Instead, we chose passivity and allowed the disconnection and division to remain. We were aware that it was there, yet were powerless to resolve it. As a result, people suffered in silence and withdrew from each other in self-protection whenever they got hurt or scared. Hurts turned into offenses, causing fear and accusation to multiply.

A CULTURE OF POWERLESSNESS

The culture of any organization, be it a church, business, or family, is set by the consistent practices and behaviors of the leaders of the organization and reinforced through the managed expectations of the people working around them. When relational disconnection and un-resolved conflict become normal, anxiety permeates the atmosphere and shapes the culture.

This was certainly the case for us. In response to this increased anxiety, our leaders tried a series of superficial fixes that ultimately did nothing to resolve the real problems. We changed our staffing and lead-ership structure multiple times, hoping this would help us move for-ward. Yet even when we made the switch from an elder-led church to a senior-pastor-led church, technically empowering Dennis to lead, we remained entrenched in the same practices. Structural and personnel changes are not enough to address the foundational issue of powerless-ness. Every change caused further disappointment as the root issues lay unaddressed, the hurt got stronger, the disconnection got deeper, the accusations built, and more people left our church wounded. We became locked in a cycle of powerlessness and passivity.

The symptoms of powerless behavior that Danny describes in his book, *Keep Your Love On*, were normal in our leadership culture when Aaron and I were on staff as youth pastors. Powerless communication styles—passive, aggressive, and passive-aggressive—characterized the conversations on the leadership team. Passive communication was the dominant style. I remember sitting through many meetings feeling like I had something to contribute, yet being too afraid to speak up out of fear of being corrected or creating an uncomfortable situation. I had seen too many examples of people getting upset and completely shutting down in meetings while the rest of us sat uncomfortably by and pretended that everything was okay. We learned by default that anything difficult was simply not spoken about, because we had never successfully navigated through disagreement or hurt. Anytime it was exposed, it only caused more pain and disconnection to be absorbed by the people involved.

There were also incidents of aggressive communication, when certain leaders or staff members got pushed too far and finally exploded with anger and accusation toward someone. Though these occurred less frequently, they happened often enough to enforce the culture of passivity through intimidation. For example, one woman told me about her experience at a planning meeting for a ministry in which she had been involved. The leader shared ideas and asked for input, but as the ministry team began to refine his ideas and propose new ones, they noticed that the leader was becoming increasingly agitated. Scared that the leader was going to explode in anger, which had happened in the past, one by one the team members shut down and eventually just agreed to everything he proposed. After the leader abruptly left the meeting, the team remained and talked about how difficult the meeting was, how much they struggled with the leader, and how some were even considering leaving the ministry. Yet none of them were ready to confront the leader about his aggressive behavior. As a result, the leader remained unaware of the impact he was having on people around him, and the team became even more entrenched in their passivity.

Another powerless behavior Danny describes in *Keep Your Love On* is triangulation—acting like a victim and blaming problems on a "bad guy" while recruiting support and protection from anyone willing to be a "good guy." This type of behavior became normal throughout our staff team. When things were difficult, we would turn to one another or to our friends outside the team for support. Office gossip was normal, and we all knew, or had a version of, what was happening behind closed doors. Together we would agree over who the "bad guy" was in the scenario, what was wrong with the church, and what needed to happen for it to be fixed.

However, we didn't even all agree on who was the bad guy! People would accuse one person while defending another person with whom they agreed. I remember conversations where staff members would share their struggles and put the blame squarely on the shoulders of one leader, saying, "I wouldn't follow him out of a paper bag." The next day, a different staff member would be accusing the other leader of taking authority that was not rightfully his and claiming that was the reason that our church could not be blessed. And of course, we had all sorts of spiritual "bad guys"—there were Jezebel spirits, Ahab spirits, Absaloms, and more!

On top of all this, we kept telling ourselves that we had a "culture of honor"! After hearing Danny's messages on honor and reading *Culture of Honor*, we had all adopted his language, often publicly saying things like, "In this house, we have a culture of honor." Yet in practice, almost none of the leadership behaviors Danny describes—creating a safe place for people to grow in freedom, driving the fear of punishment out of the culture, courageously confronting issues and empowering people to clean up messes, etc.—were visible on our team. Instead, we used "honor" as an excuse for continuing to be passive about confronting the hard issues.

BECOMING POWERFUL

After so many years of operating in this powerless culture, our first step towards becoming powerful came about almost by accident, but the timing couldn't have been more crucial! Dennis invited Tony Stoltzfus, a leadership coach from California, to do a workshop with our team. The timing of the workshop just happened to come after my appointment as finance manager and shortly after I had begun the process of communicating about our financial crisis with Dennis and the other senior leaders.

None of us really knew what to expect from working with Tony—he had simply come highly recommended to us by a couple in the church who were hosting a separate business workshop with him. Little did we know that he was about to lead us into a moment of truth that would shake things up and make way for some dramatic and life-saving changes in our organization.

As it was his first time meeting our team, Tony opened the workshop by asking a series of questions designed to get to know each of us and the experiences that had prepared us for our calling and role as leaders. It didn't take long for him to discover that the relational dynamics on our team were strained, to say the least. Most of us were avoiding eye contact with each other and offering shallow, evasive answers that made it painfully obvious we were highly uncomfortable being vulnerable with each other. Instead of backing away from our discomfort, however, Tony leaned into it, asking probing question after probing question in a quest to get to the bottom of what was going on. It became clear that he was a master at reading body language and facial expressions, and was more than happy to confront each of us with the messages we were communicating, whether intentional or not.

When it was my turn to respond to a question, Tony immediately pointed out that my body language switched to a defensive posture as I was giving my answer, and invited me to share what was actually going through my mind. I ventured a bit more honesty, hoping that would satisfy him. Instead, he told me that a scared expression had flashed across my face, and urged me go even further in sharing my thoughts and feelings. This time, I was honest to the point of tears. From then on in the meeting, my defenses and filters were down, and I became a lot more vocal and blunt in my responses. This, of course, was exactly what Tony was going for. He repeated the same process with each person in the room, pushing us to own the reality that had been in place for a long time: as a team, we were very disconnected and had no idea how to tell each other the truth of what was going on inside us. Lowering our walls was awkward and scary.

Finally, right before we stopped for lunch, one staff member said in frustration, "I wish we could just be honest with each other!"

Tony looked around the room and asked, "How many other people feel like that?" Most of the team indicated their agreement.

When we came back from lunch, we found Tony standing behind a table spread with cards labeled with different words.

"After this morning, I've decided we should wait on going through the material I had prepared for this afternoon. I want to see if I can help you start to get more honest as a team. These are emotion cards," he said, gesturing at the cards on the table. "I want each of you to choose the card that best describes how you feel in this environment."

Then Tony picked up one of the cards and turned to me. "Carla, you take this one." With that, he handed me a card that said, "Angry."

Obediently, I took the card and watched as the rest of the team made their way forward to choose one for themselves. Everyone hesitated as they sought the card that best represented their feelings. Finally, we all had our cards and stood around the room holding them up for the room to see.

Without exception, every senior leader and staff member was holding a negative emotion card. I was, as instructed, holding "Angry" and feeling very uncomfortable as I realized for the first time how truthful that was. Tony had recognized the frustration that had been leaking out in my comments all morning. Across the table from me, two of our senior leaders were holding "Inadequate" and "Sad," and one of our administrative staff was holding "Disconnected."

One by one, Tony invited each person to explain their card. Tears began to flow as team members began to tell each other the truth about their experience on the team, many of them for the first time. The problem was now out in the open, and we had taken the first step toward building trust—engaging in a vulnerable exchange of truth about what was happening inside of us.

Following Tony's workshop, due to the depth of pain that had been revealed, we invited Will and Leslie VanHook up from Montana to do counseling and Sozo ministry sessions with all the senior leaders and staff. Everyone agreed to this, and many people on the team ended up having powerful personal breakthroughs where they confronted the fears at the root of their powerless behavior. However, others on the team were less eager to engage in any kind of process of self-discovery or inner healing that would help them, and the rest of us, grow in becoming more powerful, connected, and healthy. This exposure of people's attitudes was even more important, in a way, than the truth that came to light in our workshop with Tony, because it showed us where our most critical area of misalignment lay. This ended up influencing some of the decisions Dennis finally made to avert the financial crisis and address the powerlessness that had brought it about. He knew that any effort to change our leadership culture would depend on having a team where everyone was willing to take ownership of this goal of personal growth.

RADICAL REORGANIZATION

To make these decisions, Dennis had to walk out his own journey to overcome areas of powerlessness in himself. Through the workshop with Tony and the follow-up work with Will and Leslie, he was able to admit that he had felt powerless and miserable within our existing culture for some time. He acknowledged places in his own history with the church where he had been hurt, and recognized that the pain of these experiences had contributed to his fear, confusion, and lack of confidence in his own ability to lead. Acknowledging these truths allowed him to start a journey of healing and self-discovery. What was the problem and what was he going to do about it?

Gradually, Dennis came to see that one of his greatest strengths as a leader had a weak side that had been compromising his ability to lead vision and culture for the church. Dennis functions as an Includer. Here's how CliftonStrengths describes this strength:

> You want to include people and make them feel part of the group. In direct contrast to those who are drawn only to exclusive groups, you actively avoid those groups that exclude others . . . You hate the sight of someone on the outside looking in. You want to draw them in so that they can feel the warmth of the group. You are an instinctively accepting person.[1]

Dennis is gifted in making others feel valuable, accepted, and part of the team. However, when it came to his need to be exclusive in choosing members of his core team to preserve unity of values and vision, he had not been able to do it, choosing instead to give everyone a seat at the table, even those in opposition to him. This had resulted in a divided, ineffective leadership team.

Dennis knew he had found the problem—he had prioritized keeping everyone happy and feeling valued at the expense of the corporate breakthrough we needed. But what was the solution? Sure, the financial situation was forcing the issue—he knew the church staff needed to downsize, which was already a painful prospect. In order to solve the real problem, however, Dennis recognized that he needed to grow in his ability to require everyone on the leadership team to be in align-

---

[1] https://www.gallupstrengthscenter.com/cms/en-us/gmj/682/includer

ment with his vision, mission, and core values. He needed to become exclusive in the right way, which meant overcoming the constraint of his strength as an Includer.

Initially, this prospect appeared so excruciating as to be impossible, and Dennis wondered if his only option was to resign as our senior leader. Then, a series of completely unconnected people outside the church, all unfamiliar with our story, began to reach out to him with prophetic words that repeated the same theme: "The Lord pointed out that you are an Includer. But He is going to show you who to exclude. It's time to choose who you are going to run with."

These words, along with the personal and corporate truths coming to light and the pressure of our financial situation, finally galvanized Dennis's courage to make some very difficult and powerful decisions to save the church and create a team who could run together with clear vision and purpose. He scheduled a number of hard conversations with individual members of his core leadership team, letting them know that he was dissolving the existing structure and letting five people go from the staff team. While it was an incredibly difficult process for him to walk through, it also was transformational for our church. Dennis had done what was needed to build and restructure his team around the leadership culture he wanted to create. Seeing him emerge as a powerful leader and decision-maker released much needed hope to the team who remained.

Dennis offered me the position of Executive Pastor on his newly restructured team, working directly under him to manage the staff, implement strategy, manage resources, and perhaps most importantly, actively establish the culture we wanted to create. He was aware we had a long road ahead of us shaping new leadership values and practices, creating stable financial practices, and rebuilding trust with the staff and congregation. Throughout the period of identifying the crisis and searching out a solution, however, we had already started to establish a pattern of honest communication and feedback, which gave me confidence that this could lead to lasting change. Excited at the possibility of what could now be created, and with the partnership of Aaron, I said "Yes" to the job.

The third person Dennis kept on his new leadership team was Marla, a founding member of the church who had started on staff as the secretary and had held leadership roles in almost every ministry of the church. She was the leader of the Sozo ministry, and as such, had continued to grow in wholeness herself, emerging as a powerful leader. In the restructuring, she stepped into the role of Family Life Pastor, overseeing small groups and the pastoral, healing, and women's ministries. Together she, Dennis, and I began the process of rebuilding the foundations of our leadership culture.

Largely thanks to Danny's teaching on powerless vs. powerful culture, we understood that the culture we were trying to leave behind was a culture of defaults—of behaviors and relational dynamics that were allowed to happen rather than being actively chosen in alignment with a set of core values. Powerless people are, by definition, not powerful in building the relational culture they want to create. Instead of fighting for things they value and love, they allow fear to drive them to protect themselves. Becoming powerful people who could build a powerful culture meant that we had to become clear on what we valued, what we would actively pursue, and what we would protect. Ultimately, it meant that we as leaders would not only have to be able to clearly articulate the values and behavior we wanted to cultivate in our organization—we would have to model them. Only our actions would create enough momentum to establish new culture norms.

Thankfully, we knew that the loyal core of our staff and congregation were ready for this cultural shift. The moment of honesty with Tony at the workshop, the subsequent Sozo sessions with Will and Leslie, and multiple conversations with staff members made it plain to us that everyone was hungry to finally close the gap between aspiring to a culture and actually behaving that culture. We all wanted to live in an environment that encouraged people to be powerful, vulnerable, honest, and willing to confront. We wanted to work with team members who valued connection and had the skills to communicate assertively, disagree respectfully, give and receive feedback, build and protect trust, clean up messes without involving punishment, and believe the best about one another. We wanted a culture with high levels of trust, safety, peace, love, appreciation, growth, and excellence.

And so, we embarked on a journey to learn how to lead in building this culture. This book is about the steps we have taken to move from powerlessness, fear, and disconnection to a culture of power, peace, and connection.

2

CONFRONTING POWERLESSNESS

After many years of serving on staff at Northgate in various capacities and under different leaders, I had observed and experienced the problems within the leadership culture, and was convinced that most of these problems were rooted in the powerless behavior and relational dynamics of the leaders. I had devoured *Keep Your Love On* and listened to Danny's talks on powerless vs. powerful people, and had been on a journey of learning to build a powerful mindset and behavior in my own life. In my mind, the clear path to fixing the culture began with having a leadership team aligned in the goal and capacity of being powerful, which I thought we now had. Thus, while I didn't expect transitioning into the role of Executive Pastor to come without challenges, I did expect that I would be capable of facing those challenges as a powerful person.

Instead, I discovered what every leader discovers when they get promoted into new levels of authority. Solutions are always simple from a distance! Moving into a position of responsibility changes everything, because it is there where you discover what it takes to make the hard decisions and execute the solutions required in that role—and the truth about your ability to do so. In my case, taking the responsibility to lead in building a powerful culture on our team immediately began to expose places of powerlessness in my own life.

BLINDSIDED BY CONFLICT

Within weeks of starting my new role, I had challenges with one of the members on the staff team. Lisa had a strong personality and had been frustrated in her position for quite some time, which made her combative in conflict. The first time I confronted her about some critical comments she had made, she exploded in anger.

"I knew it! I knew it wasn't safe around here! You asked me for my honest feedback, I gave it, and now I am in trouble. I will never be that honest again. In the future, don't bother asking me what I think. Clearly, you don't want to know!"

I was stunned and completely unprepared for Lisa's reaction. In my naiveté and enthusiasm for this new culture we had agreed to create, I was not prepared for such resistance to feedback. In my shock, I didn't see that her anger was really a cover for a deep place of hurt. So, instead of exploring the hurt while setting boundaries and expectations around our communication, I immediately started backpedaling.

"No, that's not true," I responded. "I want feedback and I want this to be a safe place. I am sorry that you don't feel heard. Let's put this behind us and start over again. What is it that you wanted to communicate?"

Unfortunately, that conversation set the tone for our confrontations from that point on. Whenever I brought up an issue with Lisa, she got aggressive, and I would back down and tried to do whatever it took to make her happy. I came out of these meetings with her feeling completely overwhelmed and confused—knowing that I didn't feel respected in our interactions, yet feeling like it was my fault, and thinking I could somehow fix the breakdown in our communication if I just said or did the right thing.

It didn't take long for me to start feeling anxious and afraid whenever Lisa was around. To avoid upsetting her, I became very careful about everything I said and did, and second-guessed anything I had communicated, wondering if I had done something wrong and if more conflict was coming. Before I knew it, I had taken the role of a victim and made Lisa my "bad guy." A victim believes that someone else is always responsible for the experience they are having in life. They react to what is happening around them while refusing to take ownership of their own choices or part in unhealthy relational dynamics. As victims do, I blamed Lisa for the anxiety I felt whenever she was around. I also blamed her for my inability to set clear boundaries around her behavior and communication. She was the problem and I needed her to change so I could have the peace I so desperately craved.

Again and again, I came home angry and upset about the latest thing Lisa had done or said that made me feel disrespected, and complained about it to my husband. He usually responded by gently pointing out places where my own weakness was evident and encouraging me to stop acting powerless in the face of her anger. Every time, I got defensive and deflected the issue straight back at her. I must have driven him crazy, as he could clearly see what I was not willing to see! I was so focused on her that I was unable to recognize how I was contributing to the problem and behaving in a way that was inconsistent with who I wanted to be. As long as I kept the focus on Lisa's behavior, I was powerless over my own emotions and experience, and powerless to change the culture of the office, even though it was now my responsibility.

UNCOVERING THE ROOT OF MY REACTION

It wasn't until I was on a phone call with Tony, who was now my leadership coach, that I had a powerful moment of self-discovery. I explained to him how I was freezing in conflict with Lisa, and struggling to think and communicate well.

"You are responding like you are afraid of something," Tony observed. "What are you afraid of? What is the worst-case scenario that could happen here?"

My initial thought was, *I am afraid of her!* But as I asked myself, "Is there something else I am afraid of here?" I realized something almost immediately.

"I am afraid of making a mistake!" I answered. "What if I set boundaries and I am wrong? What if she gets hurt and it's my fault? What if I destroy her by using my authority incorrectly?"

"Where did you learn to be afraid of that?" Tony asked. "Have you seen something like that happen before?"

"Yes! It happened to me!"

Suddenly it became clear. My own painful experience of working for a leader who had used anger to control the people around him was at the root of my struggle. Whenever someone tried to give this leader feedback about how they were experiencing him, he exploded in anger, and often retaliated by leveling accusations at the person and attacking their character. Eventually overwhelmed with the intensity of his reaction, the person would withdraw and leave the interaction hurt and afraid. The message repeatedly communicated was, "Your feedback is not welcome here," which resulted in broken relationship after broken relationship and was the source of a lot of pain within the team.

That experience had left me terrified of becoming a leader like that—someone who silences people trying to give me feedback, refuses to learn how people are truly experiencing me, and creates an unsafe, disconnected, and anxiety-filled culture on my team. Yet now, my fear of becoming a powerless leader was leading me to act like a powerless victim with my staff member! My reaction to who I didn't want to be was backfiring—as fear reactions always do.

The irony in this situation was not lost on me as I finally recognized what was going on. For years, I had been learning to recognize powerless and powerful attitudes and behavior. That angry leader was only one of many powerless leaders I had observed who were both completely unaware of the effect that they were having on other people and apparently uninterested in—if not resistant to—self-discovery. These experiences had impressed on me that a defining trait of every powerful leader is a high value for and practice of self-discovery and self-awareness, which had motivated me to start pursuing these in my own life. Yet I still lacked understanding of how much my own fear of being a leader who lacked self-awareness was affecting me and those around me!

Thankfully, the moment I became aware of my behavior and where it was coming from, I was able to start charting a course to change. Self-awareness opened the opportunity for me to stop being powerless and start making powerful choices.

THE ROOTS OF POWERLESSNESS: FEAR AND SELF-PROTECTION

As Danny describes in *Keep Your Love On*, the shift from a powerless to a powerful mindset is the shift from operating with an external locus of control to an internal locus of control. That is, we move from the belief that everything around us is more powerful than we are, which leads us to live in reaction to our circumstances, to the belief that we always have the power to choose how we will respond to our circumstances, which leads us to live with "response-ability" for managing our internal reality and choices:

> Powerful people do not try to control other people. They know it doesn't work, and that it's not their job. *Their job is to control themselves.* As a result, they are able to consciously and deliberately create the environment in which they want to live . . . Powerful people are not infected or affected by their environment. *They refuse to be victims of others.*[1]

The only way to make this shift is to commit to the process of self-discovery so we can grow in self-awareness. Self-awareness is where we learn to identify what is happening on the inside—our thoughts, emotions, and needs—and the experience we are creating on the outside—our behavior and its effects on the people around us. Gaining self-awareness creates the foundation for us to use our reason and will

---

[1] Danny Silk, *Keep Your Love On* (El Dorado Hills, CA: Loving on Purpose, 2013), 25-26.

to decide what to do and do it—that is, to make powerful choices about how we will respond to situations rather than mindlessly reacting to them.

The challenge in this journey is that it involves repeatedly confronting the root of powerlessness in our hearts: fear. Specifically, because we live in a fallen world where, starting in childhood, we all experience various types and degrees of relational pain, we all carry instinctive, fear-driven reactions—fight, flight, or freeze—that get triggered when we encounter the threat of more relational pain, whether that threat is real or imagined.

The first problem with these reactions is that they're instinctive, which means that they don't require active awareness to shape our thinking and behavior. If we never stop to reflect on what we're feeling and choosing and why when we're in fear, these reactions become programmed as subconscious habits in our thinking and behavior. The second and much bigger problem is that these fear-driven reactions all have the same goal—self-protection—which is fundamentally at odds with the primary goal of love and relationships—connection. Danny explains:

> The question at stake is how you will react to the pain you experience in relationships. If you fall back on the classic fear-driven reactions, you will necessarily start treating people like rattlesnakes. You will either run away or try to control people so they won't hurt you. The problem is that neither of these options will help you pursue and protect the goal of connection in a relationship.

> Unfortunately, many people grow up in relational cultures that used "rattlesnake" tools to deal with pain and the fear of pain—tools that control, manipulate, remove freedom, threaten, and withhold love. These are the tools of powerlessness.[2]

---

[2] *Keep Your Love On*, 48.

If we hope to be powerful people who can develop healthy, powerful relationships, we must develop trained responses that enable us to keep our love on and protect relationships when scary and painful things happen. Fear is the enemy of love. Love cannot grow when fear is present. Scripture says, "There is no fear in love; but perfect love casts out fear, because fear involves torment. But he who fears has not been made perfect in love."[3] Fear creates a torment of the mind, the anticipation of punishment. The anticipation of punishment will cause us to live defensively, constantly projecting and then protecting ourselves from an expected negative outcome. Torment comes from the tormentor—the devil—who delights in inflicting pain as he wars against love. If we are going to build strong relational cultures in our families and workplaces, we must be people who overcome our own fears and walk in love to drive fear and the tormentor out of our relationships.

SEEKING SELF-AWARENESS

The first step to replacing our fear reactions with loving responses is to gain self-awareness of where we default to fear, powerlessness, and self-protection in the face of relational pain. It's safe to say that most all of us have habits of self-protection in our lives. We have learned to avoid vulnerability and hide places of imperfection that could invite rejection. We push people away when we feel threatened, or refuse to take risks so we don't make mistakes that attract punishment. We may compromise healthy boundaries and become a "yes" person to avoid disappointing anyone. Or we may use anger to control others in a situation to get our needs met. When points of struggle or disagreement inevitably occur, we disconnect either physically by leaving the relationship, or emotionally by retreating behind walls we have put up in our heart.

For example, both Aaron and I came into our marriage with well-developed systems of self-protection. My default was to avoid conflict at all costs, so I would apologize for anything and everything at the smallest hint of disagreement. But my "Sorry" was not a true apology—it was

---

[3] 1 John 4:18 NKJV

simply my first line of defense to make conflict go away. This created intense frustration for him when he would bring things to me that he was struggling with, hear an apology, but see no heart shift in me. His self-protection was to escalate in arguments and be almost lawyer-like in his communication and defense, to the point that I would feel shut down and devalued in what I was thinking and feeling. Our attempts to work through conflict often caused us to become more isolated from one another and added to the growing frustration we each felt in the relationship. As we added children to the mix, it put more pressure on our marriage.

Finally, an intense season of disconnection, and the pain it caused, brought the initial awareness we needed to realize that our behavior in conflict was a serious problem that was threatening the future of our relationship. At that point, we decided to go after further discovery so we could understand why our behavior was dysfunctional and where it was coming from. This paved the way for us to pursue healing from the experiences that had originally planted these self-protective behaviors in our lives, and to actively build new skill sets for managing ourselves and protecting our connection when we had a disagreement. We have now come to the place where we can work through conflict with respect and understanding and come out the other side with a deeper connection.

In fact, the progress I had made learning to be powerful in conflict in my marriage had fueled my confidence that I would be able to do the same when I stepped into my Executive Pastor role. So, it was especially frustrating to find myself struggling in conflict with Lisa. Once I started to gain greater awareness of the dynamics in that situation, however, I recognized that there was a key difference in the two scenarios.

In my marriage, Aaron and I were equally committed to the same goal of a thriving, happy marriage. Mutually choosing the goal of connection meant that once we saw how our self-protective behaviors were hurting our connection, we went to work surrendering them and learning to behave in ways that protected "us." Sharing the same goal created safety and automatically helped to lower our anxiety around conflict.

In my new leadership role, however, I hadn't yet established that everyone on my team shared the goal of connection. One of the things my fear reaction demonstrated was that I wasn't fully prepared to pursue that goal and respond powerfully when a team member started throwing out strong self-protective behavior and consistently demonstrating that her goal was not connection. This situation challenged me to grow to a new level in my ability to be powerful in the face of another person acting powerless.

COURAGE TO LEARN THE TRUTH

As my experience with Lisa illustrates, gaining self-awareness means going from "I don't know that I don't know" to "I know that I don't know." It means opening ourselves up to experiences that lead us to moments where we say, "Wow, I had absolutely no idea that that was the experience I was creating for you. I had no idea that fear and pain and self-protection were in there." In other words, it means positioning ourselves to learn new truths about ourselves from the "mirrors" around us—God and others. And these truths are often uncomfortable. This is why, like every powerful choice, choosing self-awareness is courageous. It's courageous to stop and face the fears driving our self-protective behavior. It's also humble and relational. It's humble to open our ears and hearts to learn and receive new insights about ourselves, and it's relational to take a position of vulnerability that says, "I need your help to see what I can't see. Tell me how you're experiencing me. What kind of environment am I creating around me through my behavior?"

One essential key to success in the journey of self-awareness is that we do our best to try to *understand* the truth about ourselves before we judge it. Many of us jump right into self-judgment when we discover truth about ourselves that doesn't agree with what we call "good" or "bad," "wrong" or "right." As a result, instead of trying to understand this truth, we descend into a spiral of berating ourselves, feeling ashamed, and wanting to hide. This immediately derails us from the path of learning and growth. We can't judge ourselves and learn at the same time. Learning actually means *repenting*—changing the way we think, judge truth, and see the world. We must choose to lay judgment aside if we hope to find the truth and allow it to change our minds and behavior.

Prior to restructuring the leadership team, Dennis had a profound experience that helped him become aware that self-judgment was holding him back from greater self-discovery and growth. In that season of transition and upheaval, he had lost many of his close friends and those he had co-labored with over the years, and was in a lot of pain due to accusation that had come against him. Some had gone as far as to label him an "abusive leader." While it was true that the church had struggled under his leadership, his heart and intentions had been pure, so any accusation that came against his motivations was particularly painful to him. As the fear of more accusation had taken hold of him, he had been reacting to it with avoidance and emotional disconnection. The level of his disconnection was affecting the team, as they could see him shut down physically and withdraw emotionally in difficult situations when they were looking to him for leadership.

During this time, he went away to a retreat for pastors who were in crisis. In a small group workshop at the retreat, each pastor was given the opportunity to tell their story. After Dennis shared, one of the other pastors in the circle asked him, "How did you deal with the anger?"

"Anger?" he responded.

"If it was me, I would have been angry," the man said.

"I didn't know it was okay to be angry!"

Up until this point, Dennis had not allowed himself to feel his anger, deeming it to be a bad or wrong emotion. However, by not acknowledging the presence of anger, he was blocked from further exploring what was happening inside his own heart. The fact that he was angry was neither right nor wrong; it was simply an indicator that something deeper was going on. As soon as these words came out of his mouth, the anger that had been present all along found its way to the surface and he allowed himself to feel it for the first time. Feeling the anger caused him to admit the pain that was behind it, which opened the door for him to pursue healing. Only after he let go of the pain did he recover his ability to be present as a leader, even in difficult conversations. This experience helped Dennis embrace the necessity of growing in self-awareness by positioning people in his life who would safely give feedback, encourage him to acknowledge his emotions, and explore where those emotions were coming from without judgment.

THREE ESSENTIAL SELF-AWARENESS PRACTICES

Here are the main features of powerless thinking and behavior that we must understand and learn to recognize:

1. Powerlessness is driven by fear (specifically, the fear of punishment/relational pain).

2. Powerless behavior typically manifests as fight, flight, or freeze.

3. Powerless behavior has the goal of self-protection.

4. The powerless mindset is characterized by a victim mentality. Everything outside is more powerful and a threat.

5. Powerless language sounds like, "I can't," "I have to," "You made me," etc.

6. The classic powerless relational dynamic is triangulation (or the cycle of irresponsibility)—blaming a "bad guy" for powerless behavior and recruiting a "good guy" to work harder on your problems than you.

There are three essential practices that help us grow in recognizing powerlessness. The first is *emotional awareness*. Emotional awareness is the ability to identify what I am feeling as I am experiencing the feeling. It is a powerful tool in self-discovery, as it keeps my focus on examining what is happening in my own heart and away from the temptation to make others responsible for my emotional state.

Emotional awareness involves two skills. The first is what I call "practicing the pause." It's the discipline of stopping, especially in the middle of difficult emotional situations, to investigate and evaluate what is happening internally. The second skill is expanding our emotional vocabulary, because awareness depends on my ability to accurately identify what it is that I am feeling with specific language. When we stop to ask ourselves, "What am I feeling right now?" we need to be able to respond with a more complex emotional vocabulary than "fine" or "angry." In any one day, we experience a vast array of emotions. "Angry" may be more accurately replaced with "frustrated," "hurt," "misunderstood," or even "betrayed." If we look deeper than "fine," we may discover that we feel happy or content, or we may feel apathetic, disconnected, or numb.

Only by accurately naming the emotion can we ask, "Why? Why am I feeling what I am feeling?" Our emotions are always indicators of what's happening at the heart level—our thoughts, beliefs, and values—but until we name them, it's very difficult to trace them back to their source. As in my story, once I specifically identified my fear as the fear of making a mistake, it allowed me to explore further and discover where the fear was coming from. Achieving emotional awareness allowed me to reach the deeper level of becoming aware of my thoughts and beliefs, which set me up to ask, "Is this thought helpful or harmful in this situation? Is this belief true or untrue?" Identifying and examining our thoughts gives us the opportunity to repent from powerless thoughts and beliefs and trade them for powerful ways of thinking (more on this in the next chapter).

The second practice of self-awareness is *checking our language*. Jesus said our words are connected to our hearts: "For the mouth speaks what the heart is full of."[4] To grow in awareness, I pay attention to the words I speak, with the goal of allowing them to reveal any places of powerlessness in my heart. I particularly stay alert for any language that reveals a victim mentality, which includes complaining, blaming, making excuses, unfavorable comparison, and expressions of defeat.

---

[4] Matthew 12:34 NIV

When we first started learning about self-awareness, we adopted a powerful habit as a team that taught us how easy it was to default into victim language rather than taking ownership for our choices and behaviors. At a staff training, one of our trainers pointed out how normal it was in our culture for people to make excuses when they were late. Excuses such as "I am sorry I am late—the traffic was really bad," while culturally normal and acceptable, were expressions of powerless language that stopped us from owning and therefore correcting the true reason we were late. As a result, we embraced the challenge to stop making excuses for being late and to commit to telling the truth. On more than one occasion, my team has heard me say, "I am sorry I am late. I had poor time management." I have heard others say, "I am sorry I am late. I did not leave early enough to account for traffic." While it seems relatively harmless, the exercise has allowed us to grow in recognizing when we are making excuses for our behavior versus taking responsibility for our choices and communicating powerfully about them.

Lastly, the third essential practice of self-awareness is *seeking and receiving feedback*— allowing others to hold up the mirror so we can see how our words and behaviors are affecting those around us. When we are truly committed to growth, we will give others permission to speak into our lives and refuse the temptation to defend ourselves from what we hear. Of course, while we can grow from almost any feedback, it is important that the people we position around us are powerful people who share the same goals of learning and growth, so any truth they do bring is communicated in love.

For our team, we engaged Tony long-term as a leadership coach to give us feedback and equip us to exchange feedback successfully as a team. His work with us at the workshop revealed he had the emotional awareness tools we needed to learn how to better identify, communicate, and resolve what was happening inside of us. Like any great coach or mentor, he was able to do this while creating an environment completely free of judgment or shame for whatever was exposed. He was truly a champion of our development. As we practiced tools of self-awareness and built trust as a team, we learned to turn to one another and ask, "I am not sure what is going on inside of me right now. Are you available to help me process?"

The transformation we have experienced in our team dynamics and culture by committing to self-discovery and self-awareness has been profound, as I hope to show in the coming chapters. But first, I want to continue with the next step in the journey of self-discovery. Achieving self-awareness of our powerless behavior and its roots in our emotions and beliefs is step one. In the next chapter, we'll look at step two: repentance and healing of the heart.

SUMMARY

1. A victim will always make someone else responsible for the experiences they are having in life.

2. The shift from a powerless to a powerful mindset is the move to the belief that we always have the power to choose how we will respond to circumstances.

3. A defining trait of every powerful leader is a high value for and practice of self-discovery and self-awareness.

4. Gaining self-awareness creates the ability to make powerful choices about how we will respond to situations rather than mindlessly reacting to them.

5. The journey of self-discovery involves confronting the root of all powerlessness in our lives—fear.

6. There are three essential practices that we must embrace to grow in recognizing powerlessness—emotional awareness, checking our language, and seeking and receiving feedback.

ACTIVATION

---

1. Take a moment to consider what is happening in your life right now. Are there any challenging situations? Places of relational struggle?

2. Have an honest look at yourself, carefully looking for victim mentalities or powerless language or behavior. Ask yourself the question, "Am I reacting in fear and self-protection, or am I responding in love?"

3. Ask Jesus to reveal any roots of fear that are being exposed through the situation. "Jesus, please show me any places where I am under the influence of fear in this circumstance."

4. Refuse to judge anything that may be revealed. Often, we are tempted to hide from the truth out of the fear of what it may mean about us. Remember, self-discovery requires courage and is the first step towards becoming powerful.

5. If fear is revealed, ask the follow-up question, "When did I learn to be afraid? Has something like that happened to me before?"

6. If something is revealed through this process, congratulations! You had a powerful moment of self-discovery. In the next chapter, we will give you the activation tools to confront and overcome fear.

3

HEALING BROKEN PLACES

My coaching conversation with Tony was where I finally gained the awareness I needed to accurately identify the problem that was causing me to freeze in conflict with Lisa. I had been aware enough to know I had a problem, which was why I had gone to Tony in the first place. I knew I wasn't behaving the way I wanted to in my confrontations with her. It was not fun to repeatedly experience being triggered by the fear of being wrong or making a mistake, slipping into "freeze" mode, and then finding it extremely difficult to process my emotions and needs, think clearly, or know how to respond in the moment. It was also extremely frustrating, after my fear and need to self-protect had calmed down, to recall all the tools I had learned about how to communicate powerfully in conflict, and realize what I ought to have said in the moment. Even though my head knew the tools, it seemed as if my heart was betraying me every time, making me incapable of being the person I wanted to be.

This experience of feeling powerless to do what we want to do and remaining stuck in dysfunctional behavior is what Danny, I, and others refer to as having a "broken place" in our lives. Something is not working right in us. But behavior modification won't solve the problem, because it's the belief systems we hold in our hearts that ultimately determine our behaviors. Proverbs 4:23 teaches us, "Above all else, guard your heart, for everything you do flows from it" (NIV). The word "heart" signifies our inner man or soul, the seat of our mind, will, and emotions. To change our broken behavior, therefore, we must address the underlying wrong heart beliefs driving it.

Through his questions and observations, Tony held up a mirror that helped me see the fear that was driving my behavior and identify the painful experiences that had initially planted that fear in my heart. Without realizing it, I had allowed the pain of my past experiences to shape my beliefs about God, myself, and others. Each of these beliefs, such as, "You will lose relationship if you make a mistake," empowered the fear and drove an overwhelming desire in me to self-protect in an unhealthy way. In order to fix this broken spot, I was going to have to receive healing for my past wounds, let go of the false beliefs that were feeding my fear, and pick up a new set of truths that would form new beliefs and behavior. Until I aligned my heart with the truth of who God is and who I am, I would not be able to overcome the fear and make the needed changes to my behavior.

FORGIVENESS AND REPENTANCE

To bring healing to the wound, Tony first invited me to step into forgiveness toward the leader who had hurt me. Until I forgave him, my heart would remain connected to the situation, allowing the pain to continue influencing my subconscious thoughts and emotions and drive a fear-based reaction. Forgiveness was the first step towards stopping being a victim, letting the pain go, and effectively saying, "You no longer have the power to shape the way I think, feel, or behave."

I began to declare my forgiveness out loud. "I forgive him for every time I felt unheard, unfairly accused, or attacked. I forgive him for the anxiety I felt whenever we needed to meet. I forgive him for demonstrating that leaders were unsafe and could not be trusted."

Tears began to flow as I released the backlog of emotions that had been attached to that situation. I released any judgment that I held against him from that season, along with any desire I had picked up for vengeance—the impulse to see him exposed or punished in some way for his behavior.

After I walked through forgiveness, Tony asked, "What are the lies you have believed as a result of that situation?"

As I began to speak out the beliefs I had learned from this experience, the lie that stood out most was that it was very easy for me to be deceived. I had come to believe that I would never know if I was deceived, and therefore that I could never trust my discernment or be sure of my thoughts or opinions. Because I did not believe I could trust myself, I was looking for everyone to be in agreement with me as a sign that I was not deceived. That is an impossible expectation in any relationship, and especially in a leadership position. In this first instance where someone thought differently than I did, I couldn't make a move because suddenly I was so unsure if I was deceived or not!

The next step Tony encouraged me to take was to repent from believing these lies by verbally breaking my agreement with them and asking Jesus to show me the truth.[1] With Tony's guidance, I made the following declarations:

"I renounce the lie that I cannot trust my discernment, thoughts, or opinions. I break agreement with that lie.

"I renounce the lie that if someone disagrees with me, it means I am deceived. I break agreement with that lie.

"I renounce the lie that I will lose relationship if I make a mistake. I break agreement with that lie."

As I brought these lies out into the open, I felt the internal shift in my thinking. All of a sudden, it seemed incredible to me that I would believe what I had been believing! I even began to laugh at some of the

---

[1] The most common understanding of "repentance" is to confess and abandon your sin and pursue a life of righteousness. While this accurately describes the journey of repentance, it's also valuable to know that the New Testament Greek word for "repentance" is *metanoia*, which means to change your mind. This speaks to the truth that we can't change our behavior without changing the way that we think and believe.

things I had believed to be true until now, because as I said them out loud they seemed so ridiculous!

Next, I asked, "Jesus, what is the truth You want to speak here?"

The first thing I sensed Him say was, "You are going to make mistakes, and I am okay with it!"

His words spoke directly to my fear of making mistakes and losing relationship as a result. It began to settle in my heart that Jesus was not afraid of my imperfection, and was not going to withdraw from me or punish me when I got it wrong. As I allowed this truth to become real to me, I was able to release myself from my own unrealistic expectations of perfection, and the fear of making a mistake began to dissolve. I suddenly had the ability to see that He wasn't asking me to be perfect in my leadership or relationships. He was looking for me to grow in humility, authenticity, and vulnerability. Those were the values He desired. Instead of hiding in fear from mistakes and imperfection, I began to desire the ability to own them, learn from them, and have the skills to clean up my messes and strengthen my relationships in spite of them. With fear gone, I had a clear vision for what love in action looked like, and the empowerment to begin to demonstrate that kind of love!

SOZO MINISTRY

The guided journey of forgiveness and repentance through which Tony led me draws heavily from the tools used in Sozo ministry. In case you're not familiar with it, Sozo is an inner healing ministry aimed at bringing wholeness to body, soul, and spirit.[2] It's based on the truth that in order to break out of powerless programming in our thinking and

---

[2] *Sozo* is a Greek word that means "saved, healed, delivered." For example, in Matthew 9:22 it reads, "But Jesus turning and seeing her said, "Daughter, take courage; your faith has made you well [*sozo*]." At once the woman was made well [*sozo*]" (NASB). In Romans 10:9 it states, "If you confess with your mouth Jesus [as] Lord, and believe in your heart that God raised Him from the dead, you will be saved [*sozo*]" (NASB). The word *sozo* represents more than just physical healing or the moment we receive salvation. It is a picture of complete wholeness in mind, body, and spirit.

behavior, we need God to bring healing to the painful experiences—rejection, loss, abuse, etc.—that originally taught us to react with fear. As long as pain continues to shape our beliefs, it will produce more pain in our lives. When pressure comes on us, that past pain will come out in our present behavior. Our behavior simply becomes the indicator that there is a place of wounding that requires healing and a belief system that needs correcting. However, we can shift out of victim mode by recognizing that even though our pain was caused by the choices of someone else, over whom we had no control, we are still accountable for how we chose to respond to that pain—and that we have the opportunity to choose something different. Instead of continuing to allow pain and fear to shape our beliefs, we have the choice to allow our thoughts to be shaped by the truth of what God says.

Understanding that our spiritual battle is in our minds, Sozo aims to get to the root of anything in our thinking that is hindering a personal connection with God and expose any lies we are believing, replacing them with truth. Jesus said, "When He, the Spirit of truth, has come, He will guide you into all truth."[3] When we connect with the Holy Spirit and invite Him to guide us into truth, we access His accurate revelation of our inner world and His power to heal our hearts and change our beliefs. This revelation and power is far superior to anything we can come up with on our own! I have seen people set free from patterns of powerless behavior they had not been able to overcome, even after years of counseling, through an hour-long Sozo session.

FROM WIMPY TO FEROCIOUS

As I mentioned, before restructuring our leadership team, we brought our friends Will and Leslie in to do individual Sozo ministry with everyone on staff. Dennis, Marla, and I, along with many staff members, experienced such powerful breakthroughs through Sozo that we made the commitment to bring them back yearly to meet with

---

[3]John 16:13 NKJV

everyone on the team. We saw that learning the tools and language of Sozo was going to be critical to our ability to overcome broken places that were holding us back from becoming powerful.

Marla's Sozo enabled her to break out of powerless thinking and behavior and shift into being powerful as a leader. Prior to receiving Sozo, she had known for a long time that she was a "wimpy leader," as she put it. She even understood some of the experiences in her background that had set her up to act timid and powerless. She had been raised as a missionary kid in a native culture where women were not powerful. The statistics for rape, incest, and sexual abuse within the culture were alarmingly high, and the message ingrained in most of the native women was, "I am a woman—you can do whatever you want to me." On top of that, her church culture required that she learned to do what was right, be who she was expected to be, and wear a mask without creating any kind of waves. She believed that as a Christian, it was her place to do everything she could to serve and please whoever the leader was, without confrontation, feedback, or even voicing disagreement. She also had a personality to be a pleaser and connector, which meant that her desire for connection and peace in her relationships led her to avoid confrontation at all costs and absorb any challenges into herself. The belief system she now recognizes she lived out of was, "I don't have a voice and I don't think I should. I am a Christian, and I am going to do what is right and I am going to serve well. I am going to do the best I can to make everything peaceful." She would also now say that living with this mindset made her miserable!

Marla's Sozo began with the question, "Is there anything that has been challenging for you lately?"[4]

"I always have challenges with learning how to be a good leader," Marla answered.

"What's the challenge?"

---

[4] In a Sozo session, the minister(s) leads you through a guided conversation with God, instructing you to ask Him certain questions, listen for His response (which may come in many forms—often words in your mind or pictures in your imagination), and report what you see and hear.

"I am afraid."

Prompted by Will and Leslie, Marla asked Jesus to show her where the fear had entered her life. Immediately, a memory came to mind from when she was a child living in the village where she grew up as a missionary. On this particular day, she had been chased by a group of boys as she was going home from school. Well aware of what happened to females in that culture, she had been absolutely terrified, running as fast as she could to get home before they caught her.

This incident had been traumatic enough that it caused her to believe the lies: "I have to run away from scary people. I am not safe or protected." She had spent the rest of her life living out of those lies—withdrawing and backing down from anyone who felt scary to her, which included most of the leaders with whom she worked!

When Marla forgave the boys who had chased her and broke agreement with the lies she had believed as a result, Marla had a powerful encounter with Jesus. She felt the fear leave her body. The truth that came in the place of lies was: "I am safe and protected. I do not need to be afraid." She also specifically sensed Jesus tell her she was *ferocious*, which was the last word she would have used to describe herself as a leader!

When Marla returned to work after the Sozo, she felt completely different, and the team quickly noticed that she was different. She began to act like a leader who had permission to have a voice and was unafraid to speak up. She started contributing her opinion in meetings and confronting people when necessary. Team members began to tell her, "You are completely different" or asked, "You have changed—what happened to you?" The shift from powerless to powerful behavior in her was visible for all to see!

TAKING DOWN THE WALLS

As I spent time processing my Sozo/coaching session with Tony regarding my situation with Lisa, the Holy Spirit reminded of the first

Sozo appointment I had with Will and Leslie, which took place a few years prior, during the season in which my husband and I were working on learning to protect connection through conflict.

One of the questions Will and Leslie had me ask in that Sozo was, "Jesus, is there a wall of self-protection I have put up around my heart?"

As I asked that question, I sensed a resounding "Yes!" and could even see, in my mind's eye, a wall forming a complete circle around my heart, with no point of entry or exit. My heart appeared to be completely walled off. Even as I saw this wall, I had the sense that I had formed this place of self-protection to keep myself from ever getting hurt by anyone. It was in that moment that I suddenly saw, with startling clarity, that whenever I was in a difficult relational situation, I would emotionally retreat and become compliant to diffuse the situation. No one could connect with my heart, because it was no longer available. My goal was not to connect to the other person, but to make the situation go away. I would either go completely silent and stare at the floor, or agree with whatever was being said and sometimes offer false encouragement, even as I was seething on the inside.

Even as I experienced this powerful realization, my mind went back to a memory from high school. I was in a situation where a number of my friends were making fun of me and calling me names, and I was asking them to stop. Their mocking was lighthearted and not malicious in nature, but as a teenage girl who was struggling with self-image at the time, it felt incredibly painful. Asking them to stop only seemed to encourage them. Finally, in desperation I turned to my best friend and begged her to make them stop, thinking she would help me. Instead, she joined them in making fun of me. I was horrified and felt completely helpless. Eventually, I just walked away in shame.

I realized that in the pain of that experience, I had taken on the belief that no one could be trusted, and that even your friends could hurt you at any time. Therefore, the logical conclusion was to wall off my heart and not allow anyone that level of access to hurt me again. If anyone made fun of me, it could bounce off my wall before it had a chance to penetrate my heart. Now, years after that event, that wall was hindering my ability to communicate truth, face conflict, and fully connect with the people around me, particularly my husband.

As Will and Leslie prompted me, I broke agreement with the lies I had been believing and I asked, "Jesus, what is the truth?"

"The truth is that you can trust Me to protect your heart. As you trust Me with your heart, I will teach you to live unafraid and fully alive."

"Jesus, is it time for the wall to come down?"

"Yes," came the gentle reply. "You put up that wall to keep yourself from getting hurt, but the wall is holding you back. It has become your own barrier. It's keeping Me on the outside, blocked from access to your heart, and it's keeping you from moving forward into the places I am calling you to go."

"Jesus, what is Your promise to me if I take the wall down?"

"I can't promise you that you won't be hurt. When we truly love, we expose ourselves to the risk of being hurt and rejected, and we cannot control that. But I can promise you that I will be with you, that I will not let it rob from you, and that I can take it all and turn it for your good!"

Choosing to break down that wall of self-protection around my heart had restored my ability to feel again, even in the middle of tense situations. I still remember the first time after that Sozo when I was in conflict with my husband and I didn't retreat emotionally and shut down like I normally would have. The number and intensity of emotions I felt was so overwhelming that I didn't know what to do with them, and language he had never heard from me was coming out of my mouth! As I discovered, being able to feel again didn't mean I automatically knew how to manage my emotions in a healthy way. But it did mean that I now had the freedom to go back and start learning how to practice skills of emotional awareness and healthy communication successfully. Before I received healing, I had learned about these skills and tools, but had never been able to make much progress with them because I was hiding behind my wall. Healing set me on a journey to form new relational habits.

As I pondered the journey I had been on since that first Sozo, the Lord brought more clarity to help me understand the significance of my current situation with Lisa. The fact that I had been reverting to self-protective behavior with her, after walking in a healthy place for years, didn't mean that I was going backwards. Yes, I had discovered that there was more healing God wanted to do in me. But the health and growth I had walked through in my marriage had prepared me for this new season of healing and growth. I had learned how to be powerful in conflict in my marriage, and now God wanted to teach me to be powerful in conflict with my team. As He had said in my first Sozo, there was never a guarantee that I wouldn't be hurt in any relationship. But His promise to protect my heart and turn all things to my good still stood firm and strong.

STEPS TO WALK IN WHOLENESS

In the same way that my first Sozo freed me to feel, but didn't instantly cause emotional maturity, the healing I received through my session with Tony didn't instantly cause me to stop freezing and start behaving powerfully in conversations with Lisa. However, getting free from the fear of making a mistake or losing relationship enabled me to do something I hadn't been able to do up to this point in my interactions with her—admit that I was struggling and ask for help. Until then, I had gone into meeting after meeting thinking I could (or that I should be able to) do it by myself. Now, I could finally admit I was in a situation that was beyond my experience or capability. As I had in my marriage, I wanted to grow and establish new habits of powerful behavior in conflict with Lisa and other team members. But I knew it wasn't going to happen overnight, and I knew I couldn't establish those habits on my own.

Once I recognized this, I decided to set a boundary—I would no longer meet with Lisa by myself. Instead, I reached out to another leader, explained the struggle that I had been having, and asked them to accompany me to my meetings with Lisa. I gave them full permission to stop me mid-meeting if I started getting defensive or behaving powerlessly, and asked for feedback afterwards. This stopped me from acting like a victim and enabled me to start building the confidence I needed to trust my discernment.

As the months unfolded, this plan proved to be effective—not in making conflict with Lisa go away, but in enabling me to get better and better at managing myself in the midst of it. Though our relationship continued to be messy and full of tension, I was able to start leveraging that tension in a productive direction that fueled rather than hindered my growth. It became more and more evident that walking through inner healing had successfully enabled me to make a fundamental and crucial shift in my whole approach to leadership. Before healing, I had been trapped by a stronghold rooted in a negative. After experiencing the pain of being treated poorly by a leader, I had never wanted to treat someone else that way. However, that unresolved pain and fear caused me to be stuck spending my energy attempting to avoid who I didn't want to be rather than actively pursuing the good of who I wanted to become. Through healing, my vision for my leadership style pivoted from "I will not be like the leader who hurt me" to "These are the values and behaviors I will demonstrate as a leader." Being freed to pursue this positive leadership identity was a huge step from powerless to powerful.

SUMMARY

1. When we feel powerless to do what we want to do and remain stuck in cycles of dysfunctional behavior, it reveals a broken place in our lives.

2. Behavior modification does not solve the problem, because it is our beliefs that determine our behaviors.

3. To fix broken places, we need to receive healing from past wounds, let go of false beliefs that feed fear, and pick up a new set of truths that form our beliefs and behavior.

4. Forgiveness is the first step towards healing.

5. The journey of healing allows us to examine the beliefs that we have picked up due to past painful experiences and exchange them for the truth based on God's Word.

6. The healing process allows us to confront and overcome fear in our lives, which enables us to become powerful in building healthy, loving relationships.

ACTIVATION

1. Revisit the activation from the last chapter. Was there any root of fear revealed to you? If nothing clear comes to mind, take a moment to ask Jesus, "Is there any place of past pain that You would like to heal me from in this season?"

2. If serious abuse, trauma, or neglect in your past has been revealed, it is very important to invite a professional trained in supporting victims of these experiences into the healing journey with you. Freedom will come far more quickly when we allow someone to lead us through the journey of healing. We recommend that you look for a trained professional in your area or ask your local church what resources they have available for help.

3. Otherwise, take a moment to ask Jesus, "Is there anyone I need to forgive in this situation?" Remember that forgiveness is the first step towards no longer being a victim and saying that past pain no longer has the power to

shape how you think, feel, or behave.

4. If anyone comes to mind, begin to release forgiveness out loud. "Jesus, I forgive this person for _____." Continue to speak out forgiveness until you have released them from every place you have held them responsible for the pain and suffering you have experienced.

5. Then ask, "Jesus, are there any lies I have believed as a result of that situation?"

6. As any lie is revealed, declare out loud, "Jesus, I renounce the lie that _____ and I break agreement with it. What is the truth You want to tell me in its place?"

7. As any lies/truth are revealed, write them down. Actively commit to continuing to review the new truths on a daily basis in order to retrain your mind out of the old, subconscious belief system and into the truth that has been revealed.

4

BECOMING A POWERFUL LEADER

When I started leadership coaching with Tony, one of the first exercises he had me do was designed to help me discover my life calling. He began by asking me questions, such as, "What do you want to be doing in ten years?" that helped me narrow down and identify some of the dreams I had for my life.

Once we had a few dreams written down, he asked, "What are the top competencies you would need for that role? What skill sets do you want to master?" Together, we made a list of the skills I would need to be successful in some of the things I dreamed of doing. From there, we identified certain areas where I could invest in learning and growth immediately, either through accessing books, classes, and resources on the topics or getting around people who were already well developed in those skill sets.

However, Tony also reminded me that the primary driver of learning and growth is experience. When I identified that one of my dreams was to help transform people and organizational cultures, Tony made the prophetic observation, "Then God is going to build in you the capacity to walk in cultures that are dysfunctional, deal with conflict, and not crumble. He will transform you first." He pointed out that I was going to have to grow in my ability to navigate difficult situations, which

51

was only going to come through working with challenging people, and learning to meet God amid those challenges.

I confess that while I faithfully wrote down Tony's words in my coaching notes, I was many months-deep into my journey of navigating conflict in my new leadership role before I realized that I was in the middle of the exact experience he had predicted! One of the reasons it took so long for me to gain this perspective was that the actual experience of dealing with conflict and working with challenging people was agonizing. It meant bringing out into the open years of unresolved disagreements and disconnection. It meant removing people from the team. It also meant people getting angry at me, hiding from me, and accusing me. In some cases, it meant broken relationships and living with the pain of not being reconciled with people I cared about. When we walk through challenging seasons, there are no guarantees that people will choose to walk with us or that our relationships will endure the testing. These experiences were all emotionally intense, draining, and simply *painful*.

POWERFUL IN THE PAIN

It's easy to lose perspective in painful seasons. That's what pain does—it draws our focus to the point of pain and causes us to do whatever it takes to make it go away. But recovering God's perspective on our pain is essential, because one of the primary themes on the journey from powerless to powerful is learning to relate to painful experiences in a new way.

After we gain awareness of our fear-driven, powerless behavior and walk through healing and repentance for how we reacted to pain in the past, the next step in the process of becoming powerful is responding to pain in a way that proves and builds strength of character. Instead of powerlessly succumbing to fear-based reactions, we must practice using the spiritual, emotional, and relational tools and disciplines that enable us to overcome fear and access the supernatural love, peace, healing, and courage we need to be powerful in painful circumstances. This is how God designed us to mature and see the fulfillment of our dreams and divine purpose.

When we look at the people in Scripture and throughout history who were specifically called by God to positions of leadership, we see that He always prepared them for those positions by leading them through all kinds of painful experiences that tested and shaped their character. God prepared Joseph to lead Egypt by leading him through years of family rejection, slavery, false accusation, imprisonment, and abandonment. Before taking the throne of Israel, David endured multiple assassination attempts, betrayals, alienation, homelessness, and years of living as a hunted man. So, it shouldn't surprise those of us who feel called to leadership when God leads us into challenging circumstances. If we choose to see them from God's perspective, those challenging situations will catalyze our best seasons of growth as we build the capacity to step into the roles we dream about.

Three years after the coaching session where Tony and I had mapped out the plan for my leadership development, we had another coaching call in which I was complaining to Tony about how hard my job was, bemoaning my challenges with certain people on the team and the loss of a personal friendship.

Tony simply responded by having me ask Jesus a question.

"Jesus, when You gave me this leadership assignment, what was Your goal for me?"

Immediately, I heard one word: "Growth."

"And how was that growth going to happen?"

"Through pressure-cooker situations, like the one with Lisa."

As I pondered that, I began to see all that had happened in me as a result of walking through that one relational challenge. An area of powerlessness had been exposed, a place of pain had been healed, fear had been confronted and overcome, and I had been pushed beyond my comfort zone in the areas of communication, confrontation, and healthy boundaries. As my mind went back through other challenging situations I had walked through, I could see with new perspective how each of them had developed something in me. All of them had stretched me and caused me to have to practice the very skill sets I had identified I needed at the beginning of my leadership journey. I also saw that getting distracted by the pain of the process had caused me to lose sight of my vision for development into who I wanted to be.

I left that conversation thankful for what God had accomplished in the previous years and full of fresh energy to say "yes" to the challenges of the moment, knowing that they were an opportunity for further development. I also made the commitment to find ways to keep re-aligning myself with the vision and the goal of growth so I could be better about recognizing the growth opportunities in front of me, especially amid difficulties.

While I am still very much on this journey of growth as a leader (Dennis and Marla would say the same of themselves), I do want to offer some insights I've gained about three core areas of powerlessness that God will lead us to overcome as He transforms us into powerful leaders: inadequacy, fear of punishment, and insignificance.

FROM INADEQUACY TO TRUST

Before I became a leader, I was under the illusion that some divine encounter, sign, or prophetic word would suddenly cause me to feel anointed, full of confidence, and ready to step into my calling. When I saw leaders I admired operate in their gifting, I truly felt that they had access to something that I did not yet have access to. I was waiting for something to happen to me so I could cross over that line. I also thought that leaders had all the answers and walked with God in such a way that things just happened around them. They just naturally knew what to do and how to do it, so they had favor with God and the people. I looked forward to crossing that line into leadership, for obvious reasons. Who would not want to operate like that?

The reality of my leadership journey stripped me of these illusions. While I did seek prophetic direction and confirmation from the Lord before agreeing to step into the Executive Pastor role, there was no encounter that suddenly transformed me into a powerful, confident leader. Instead, I found myself with the task of overseeing a struggling staff, managing the church finances after near-bankruptcy, and trying to build strategy for reforming a culture fraught with dysfunction and painful history. I had no idea what to do or where to start. I was truly over my head.

Instead of confidence, a fresh insecurity emerged as I was confronted with my own inadequacy. I wasn't prepared to find myself in situations where I was unsure of myself, facing questions that I didn't have answers to. I had a lot of decisions to make and I was aware that my decisions would affect everyone in the organization and potentially the success of the church. I also knew that no matter what decisions I made, it was impossible to keep everyone happy. I wanted to appear strong and confident, to have success quickly and gain the trust of the staff. Yet soon I reached the point where I was questioning if I could even do what I had signed on to do.

One of the first times I saw my insecurity flare up was when one of our department heads stopped by my office for a few minutes to ask me some questions.

"Can you tell me about your business model?" she asked.

"What do you mean?" My mind was racing. To be honest, I didn't really understand the question, but I didn't want her to know that. While I had a degree in business and years of experience in financial management, I had no experience developing or executing business models.

"What kind of business model does the church use to make financial decisions?" She then mentioned a couple of examples of different churches or nonprofits she had seen who had a defined business model that enabled them to make strategic decisions with their resources.

I felt challenged and started to get defensive. I was managing the finances. It was my department, not hers. Was she suggesting that I wasn't doing a good job? Was she suggesting that I wasn't being strategic in my decision making? How dare she! I replied very sharply and shut the conversation down, making it clear that it was my area of expertise and her input was not welcome. The conversation didn't last five minutes before I had driven her out of my office with my response.

It took about thirty minutes before I calmed down enough to go, "What just happened?" I recognized that she had asked some great questions, but because I hadn't fully understood them, I had started to feel stupid and insecure in an area where I was usually the expert. Rather than admit that I didn't really know anything about business models or strategic financial planning, I chose to preserve my place as "king" over the finances by shutting her down. In doing so, I also chose to keep up an appearance of strength rather than be vulnerable and keep my heart open to new thoughts and ideas that could help me improve.

I quickly repented and reached for the phone. "I am sorry for getting defensive when you asked about the business model," I told her. "I really want to hear more about what you have to say. Can we set up a time to talk about it?"

As I started to bring these moments of insecure behavior before the Lord, I recognized that yes, in one sense I was inadequate for the role I had stepped into. God had led me past the place where I could function comfortably and confidently as an expert with my current level of skills and resources and achieve manageable outcomes. This presented me with a choice. Would I own my inadequacy and embark on a learning journey, trusting that God would make me adequate? Or would I continue to try to rely on my own strength, skills, and resources—while attempting to hide my inadequacy and project a false image of confidence to those I was leading?

Proverbs 3:5-7 says, "Trust in the Lord with all your heart and do not lean on your own understanding. In all your ways acknowledge Him, and He will make your paths straight. Do not be wise in your own eyes; fear the Lord and turn away from evil" (ESV). This is the choice before all of us—either to rely on God or ourselves. When we "lean on" our own strength, gifts, and abilities, we insist on defining what is expected of us and striving to meet those expectations. This is how we end up in the realm of performance. When we operate out of performance, we are constantly measuring ourselves by our own expectations, and any place of weakness or shortfall becomes a source of perceived failure and shame. In turn, shame leads us hide. It keeps us from admitting our weakness, saying "I don't know," or asking for help, and drives us to keep up an appearance of having it all together. This is the reality of becoming "right in our own eyes," which, according to Proverbs 12:15, is the "way of a fool" (NKJV).

Signs and symptoms of operating from performance can include:

1. An absence of joy and peace

2. A constant drive to achieve more

3. A constant sense that I am falling short of where I should be, not measuring up to my own expectations

4. An instinctive reaction to hide mistakes

5. A need to have all the answers

6. A struggle to admit "I don't know" or ask for help

7. Resistance to coaching or counsel

8. Defensiveness when people ask questions or offer advice

9. Offense at negative feedback

10. Struggle to delegate or work with a team

When we choose not to rely on ourselves but God, however, we "acknowledge Him" in all our ways. To acknowledge Him indicates a place of intimate knowledge, as *The Passion Translation* puts it: "Become intimate with Him in whatever you do." This means that we allow Him both to define the expectations for our lives and empower us to fulfill them. This trains our minds to recognize that there is a way higher than our ways, thoughts higher than our thoughts, and a source of strength that is available in our weakness. Areas of inadequacy are not causes for condemnation and shame, but places where we find Him inviting us to move beyond the limitations of our own ways, thoughts, and strength by accessing His. We are set free to walk in the truth, to be real about our struggles and needs and move toward God and others without needing them to see us in a certain way. We can also rest in the knowledge that He is the one who "makes our paths straight"—who causes hard things to become easy, releases peace into chaos, and makes us successful in what He has called us to do.

The test of trust is a permanent fixture in the life of every leader. As long as we follow God, He will continue to lead us out of our comfort zones, past our limitations, and into realms where we can learn, grow, and be transformed. As we experience success, get promoted, or come into new places of favor and opportunity, it is normal for new insecurities around our inadequacy to appear. The source of our trust gets tested again, and at a new level, because we have something precious to lose. If we're not careful, the fear of losing what we just gained will cause us to come under the pressure to perform and attempt to pull success into the realm that we can control. Whenever we take on the need to control the outcome, we are putting our trust in our own strength, gifts, and abilities. Getting our eyes off the ways and nature of God and back onto ourselves and our abilities to achieve makes us forget that the trust that got us to this new position has the power to keep us there.

I have worked with people who were incredible, faithful leaders in the church. Everything they were part of thrived. People were constantly drawn to them and came alive around them. When they were promoted into higher levels of leadership, it was the obvious choice that everyone celebrated. However, after a while something became different. They stopped receiving feedback from those around them, including their closest friends. They stopped asking input from the team into any decisions that were made. The only voice of influence they allowed in their life was from other leaders who lived in different states and weren't positioned to see and give advice on the day-to-day situations they were facing. They shut down and drove away anyone who disagreed with them with questions like, "Are you the one who has been anointed as leader over this? No? Well, I am!" Where they had once been team players, they began to behave like sovereign kings. Things that used to thrive under their influence began to get stifled and die off. Powerful, talented people left their team and moved on to other ministries. The test of promotion caused their lives to shrink rather than to expand. This is why it is so crucial that as the Lord entrusts us with more, we commit to trusting Him at a deeper level.

FROM THE FEAR OF PUNISHMENT TO PEACE

One morning, about two years into my tenure as Executive Pastor, I woke up with the overwhelming feeling that I didn't want to go to work. I found myself wishing I was sick so I had a reason to stay in bed! This was not at all normal for me, so I knew there was something going on in my heart. I started to ask myself some questions with the coaching tools I had learned.

"Right now, you don't want to go to work. What is it that you want?"

The thought that immediately came to mind was, *I want to crawl into a cave and hide!*

"Why? What would that give me?'

Straight away, I knew what I was trying to avoid. We were in a season where multiple relationships among the staff and leadership team were being challenged. I had recently been involved in several confrontations and hard conversations that had taken a lot of emotional energy, and I knew that more would be happening soon. Just that week, I had been informed of a conflict between two team members that had not been resolved and was escalating. It appeared as if one team member was being very dishonest, necessitating my intervention. Aware that this team member was also given to angry outbursts, I knew the confrontation could get ugly and that I had to be prepared to communicate some clear boundaries and perhaps even introduce some consequences. The heart reaction I woke up to that morning was because everything in me wanted to avoid the conflict.

I found myself saying out loud, "I am so sick of being the bad guy!"

As I considered what that meant, I realized that I was tired of initiating hard conversations that had the potential to upset people. The thought that immediately followed was, *I just want people to like me. I want to be the leader that is loved by everyone.* I was picturing what would happen if I upset this person and they told their family members and friends, all people who were very involved in the church. It was a very real possibility that I could lose favor with a group of people over this situation. The fear of not being liked was causing me to want to run and hide.

In that moment, I had a choice. I had no control over the outcome of the situation because I cannot control the response of another person. They could choose to get angry and make me the bad guy. They could choose to take that complaint to their family and friends. It could change the way a group of people thought about me. Yet if I lived controlled by the fear of that outcome, I knew I would be ineffective as a leader. I cannot lead people well if I am driven by a need for them to like me or even agree with me.

I chose to take the fear to Jesus.

"Jesus, I am afraid that if I do this, a whole group of people might not like me as a result."

"They might not. Welcome to the club!" I sensed His smile in the answer.

Straight away, my mind went to scenes from the New Testament. The crowd gathering to listen to Jesus teach and then later picking up stones to kill him (John 8). A large group of disciples following Him who left when they didn't like His teaching (John 6). A triumphant entry into Jerusalem followed by a crowd chanting, "Crucify Him!" (John 12, 19).

"Jesus how did You do it? How did You so confidently make choices that You knew would result in rejection?"

"I knew whose approval I was living for. When you live in the pleasure of the Father, you don't have to go looking for it from men."

"So, what do You approve of in me?"

"I love that you take no delight in conflict and confrontation, yet when it is required, you will follow Me there."

Seeing the confrontation ahead of me as something Jesus was leading me into brought a significant shift in perspective for me. Confrontation was not just my job responsibility—in this situation, it was how I was called to partner with Jesus in building the culture of His house. Understanding that invited resolve and courage to get out of bed and prepare myself to willingly step toward the hard conversations. However, I sensed that there was still more internal work I needed to do to make sure I went into the day's meetings with my heart and mind free from fear and aligned with love and truth.

"Jesus, is there a lie I am believing?" I asked.

The immediate thought that came to mind was, "I can't be okay if someone is not okay with me."

"Jesus, can You show me where I took on that belief?"

A memory immediately came to my mind. Many years before, I had been a volunteer on a ministry team at a different church. I wasn't aware of the full expectations that came with the position, and apparently hadn't been meeting them for quite some time. I was expected to arrive earlier and stay later than I had been. One day, when I again arrived later than expected, the frustration that had been building up in the leader came exploding out. In front of several other people, she harshly told me how I was failing and what was wrong with me. I was so embarrassed and hurt that I spent the rest of the night fighting off tears. While I corrected my behavior, that leader distanced herself from me and our relationship was never the same again. As I recalled the situation and felt the emotion, I was surprised because I had not thought about it or even remembered it in a long time. It amazed me that a belief I took on in that moment could still be affecting my relationships today, even long after the memory and the hurt had faded.

I started to release forgiveness. "Jesus, I forgive her for the embarrassment I felt in that moment. I forgive her for the harsh words she said to me and I forgive her for the unfair accusations. Jesus, I also forgive her for distancing herself from relationship with me and making me feel punished for not meeting her expectations."

Next, I went back and asked, "Jesus, are there any other lies I took on because of that situation?"

The Holy Spirit began to show me that I had taken on the belief that if someone was upset at me, it would always end badly, that I would be punished in some way. I also believed that it would come unexpectedly, so I had to constantly be on my guard and anticipate what that punishment would look like because it could happen at any moment. As I was anticipating punishment, I would subconsciously try to avoid it before it could happen. If I suspected someone was upset at me, I would do anything in my power to smooth over the relationship. The cycle of fear and torment was keeping me from being free and bringing my full self into relationships.

As I confessed the fear of punishment and the lies I had been believing, I asked Jesus, "What is the truth?"

I sensed Him speaking, "You and I will always be okay. If that's true, then you are okay even when others are upset. The truth is that in healthy relationship, conflict can have a redemptive end!"

A tool that we often use in inner healing ministry is the divine exchange. We take the place of struggle to Jesus and fully release it to Him, allowing Him to replace it instead with what He has available for us. You see the idea in Isaiah 61:3: ". . . to give them beauty for ashes, the oil of joy for mourning, the garment of praise for the spirit of heaviness" (NKJV).

I offered the fear to Jesus for Him to exchange. "Jesus, I bring you this fear and I fully release it to you. Is there something You have for me in return?"

"Peace. You and I are okay, and we have a whole new adventure to go on from that place!"

After handing over the fear and inviting a new truth to be established, I was aware that the real work lay ahead of me—practicing the truth that peace, not the fear of punishment, could now reign in my heart no matter what relational situation I was facing. Fear had dominated that part of my life for so long that I would have to purpose to build and strengthen a new reality of peace in my heart until it became normal practice. I needed to continue to allow His love to cast out fear so I could consistently reject all need for approval and anticipation of punishment as influences in my mind and heart, and grow in the confidence that I will be okay no matter what the people around me do.

FROM "NOT ENOUGH" TO SIGNIFICANT

Researcher and author Brené Brown, PhD notes in her book *Daring Greatly* that many people struggle with a "shame-based fear of being ordinary."[1] The desire and need for significance is hidden in all of us. This is simply a desire to be a part of something bigger than ourselves, to have impact, leave a legacy, or achieve something with our lives. It is a healthy, God-given desire. However, this desire becomes a source of shame when we live more aware of our own insignificance than of our worth. Most people live believing that they are not enough—not smart enough, successful enough, attractive enough, (you fill in the blank) enough—so they are falling short of the greatness they dream of. They fear living an ordinary life with nothing about them that would cause them to stand out.

When we live out of insignificance, we will attempt to build success in our own strength, and according to the world's definition of success, to fulfill the desire we carry for greatness. We aim for position and promotion, bigger houses, nicer cars, and bigger paychecks. We want to be friends with all the "right" people, to be good at something, or be the

---

[1] Brené Brown, *Daring Greatly: How the Courage to Be Vulnerable Transforms the Way We Live, Love, Parent and Lead* (New York, NY: Penguin Random House, 2012), 22.

expert in the room—all to prove to ourselves and others that we are somebody of worth and value.

Growing up, our family did not have a lot of money. My father worked hard and budgeted well to make sure all our needs were met, but we didn't have the money for all the extra things that his four daughters desired. The high school I attended required us to wear school uniforms that were a disgusting shade of brown and gold. For me, the uniforms were a relief because I didn't own clothing that was popular at the time. However, once a month, our school would host a "mufti day" where we could wear our normal clothes to school. As you can imagine, everyone turned out in their best clothes that day. Most kids loved mufti day, but I always dreaded it, because on that day it was exposed that I did not measure up.

One year, my only winter shoes were the brown shoes required as a part of my school uniform, which meant that even on mufti days I still had to wear my uniform shoes to school. I still have a clear memory of the day when even my friends made fun of me for wearing those ugly brown shoes. It seems ridiculous now that a pair of shoes would matter that much, but at the time I was mortified. I could feel myself shrinking in shame.

From the experiences I had during those years, I took on the belief that wearing the right clothes and owning the right things would make me more significant and cause me to have more value in the eyes of other people. When I left high school and went into the workplace, I carried my "not enoughs" with me, and I was determined to prove to the world that I was somebody! Among other things, this caused me to be very driven in my career. My goal was promotion and the power and money that came with it. I worked hard, moved up the ranks quickly, and spent my money as fast I earned it.

The problem was it was never enough to satisfy that broken place. I constantly bought new clothes, and for a moment I would feel good about myself for looking the part. But as soon as I had worn them once, the shine would wear off and I couldn't get that feeling back. I applied for credit cards and got into debt so I could feed the constant need to have new and expensive things. I didn't feel confident going to social events unless I was wearing brand-new clothing and dripping in gold jewelry, proving to everyone around me that I was doing well for myself.

At the time, I wasn't consciously aware that my spending was driven by a deep-seated belief of insignificance. It wasn't until I took some time away to attend Youth with a Mission that the emptiness of my world and the lie driving it were exposed. I found myself in a completely new environment based on a different value system. I no longer had a position of management that caused people to respect me or a salary that proved that I was successful. Without the salary, I ran out of money quickly and couldn't keep up my spending habits. I was officially a poor missionary! As my insecurities came to the surface, I discovered that I had been hiding behind all the external things I had built, believing they gave me value. When they were taken away, the true me that desperately desired significance but lived only aware of my insignificance was revealed.

It was into that place that God spoke—an encounter that was the beginning of a lifelong journey of discovering and believing the truth of what God says about my identity as His child. "I don't need a reason to love you," He told me. "If I need a reason, then as soon as that reason is taken away, My love goes too. I just love you—no strings attached."

The Lord also began to help me see the clear fruit of a life lived out of the worthiness of our identity in Him versus a life lived striving for significance. Very simply, those who are secure in their identity and worthiness serve others, while those striving for significance serve themselves. This is why Jesus said that the kingdom measure of greatness was to be a servant (Mark 10:43). When we become free from the lie of insignificance, it is proven in our ability to serve others. If we don't derive value from what we do or the position we have, then it releases us to put value on others through serving them.

As Jesus taught and demonstrated, the art of leadership is all about serving people well. Every leader who hopes to lead effectively and build a healthy culture must settle any broken places of insignificance in their heart so we can serve others and avoid making our role about us. Here are some signs and symptoms of leadership based on the drive for significance, versus leading from significance:

1. You consistently sacrifice other priorities such as family for the sake of your work.

2. You consistently work more than your expected hours in the week, often skipping lunch or coffee breaks.

3. You don't take regular, restful vacations or personal retreats.

4. You feel as if the people around you often fail to meet your expectations. You expect everyone to be as driven and committed as you.

5. You have very little tolerance for people who make mistakes or who think differently than you. They feel like a threat to your success.

6. You believe that the organization could not be successful without you. This thought is a source of pride/satisfaction.

7. When you reach a goal or a dream, you don't stop to celebrate—you immediately move on to the next thing.

8. You do not invest in training others and giving them the opportunity to learn your job.

9. You take negative feedback about your church/organization/department personally, resenting that people don't understand your level of sacrifice.

10. You have tied your sense of personal success to the success of the organization you work for.

Even after the encounter I had in my YWAM training, I continued to struggle with layers of the insignificance lie. Any time I entered a new environment or role, I found that my "not enoughs" wanted to come racing back. When my sense of insignificance was triggered, I could quickly be overtaken by the desire to be the expert in the room, to be well loved, and to get the attention of people I admire. I would start viewing people as either a threat or a contributor to my significance, and treating them accordingly.

One of the early times this came up in my new leadership position, I was extremely frustrated with someone on the team. I felt like they weren't doing their job properly, and I was preparing myself to go and tell them! Thankfully before that happened, I vented my frustration to Tony in a coaching session. Tony had already worked with me long enough to know that when strong emotions of anger or frustration were being triggered in me, it was usually because, subconsciously, I felt my significance was under threat. He suggested that I needed to explore why I felt so frustrated and responsible to fix this person rather than having the clarity to look at whether there was a good reason for the way they were functioning. People always do things for a reason, and if I can find the reason, I can solve the problem. If I am just reacting to them in my frustration, I lose my ability to see them clearly and risk creating a bigger problem if I communicate out of my anger.

Once again, Tony led me through asking Jesus some questions.

"Jesus, is there something here that I am afraid of?"

Immediately after I asked that question, I had the realization that I believed that this person was threatening the success of the church. As Tony took that line of questioning further, I realized that I had attached some of my significance to my role in the church. So by threatening the success of the church, this person was also a threat to my personal success and significance. That belief was driving the intense frustration I had towards them, which was why I felt such a strong desire to correct their behavior.

As I again confessed this lie and sought to re-establish the truth of my significance, Tony led me in some more questions.

"Jesus what did I do today that was significant to You?"

"You showed up." I took some time to let that hit my heart.

"Jesus if this church never succeeds, if all that I am working towards fails, how is my life significant to You?"

I have had to ask some version of that question repeatedly over the last three years, and every time the answer comes back something like:

"You don't need anything to succeed to be significant to Me. Even if everything fails, I love that you walk with Me. I love this journey that we are on."

I have discovered that I need to hear this repeatedly to actively re-wire the pathway of my mind. When we grow up believing we are insignificant, "not enough," and needing to prove our worth, it stays the default way of thinking, especially in moments of vulnerability. It takes time and effort to establish a new way of thinking until it becomes the default. Even as I was having encounters and hearing the truth, I was running into the same struggle as I was presented with new situations. I was increasingly frustrated as it came up again and again. I wanted it to be settled in one transaction!

I intentionally began to create a reservoir of truth to have on hand to draw from when I encountered situations where insignificance is triggered. To do that, I set up stopping points in each day with the idea to connect to the heart of Jesus. Even now, after doing this for almost three years, I have an alarm on my phone that goes three times a day that reminds me to take a pause and meditate on truth. I will stop, close my eyes, and ask some simple questions.

"Jesus, remind me what it is You like about me?"

"Jesus, what does success look like to You?"

"Jesus, what do You want to tell me today?"

"Jesus, what makes me significant to You?"

"Jesus, is there someone I can put value on today?"

As I have practiced and reviewed the truth about who I am and where my worth comes from, it has settled deeper and deeper into my heart. The times when insignificance is triggered have become fewer and farther between and I am much quicker to identify it when it happens. I am now more aware of my own emotional reactions and much quicker to run back to Jesus when I feel shaky. Living settled that I am enough sets me free to begin to see value in the lives of others, to desire their greatness to be fully released, and to serve them towards that journey.

CONCLUSION

The theme in all these shifts—from insecurity to trust, fear of punishment to peace, and insignificance to significance—is that we are learning to respond to relational pain from security in our identity and relationship with Christ. We are growing in our ability to consistently access the power inside us that is greater than anything outside us. This is the only solid rock upon which to build a powerful life and become a powerful leader—the reality of who He is to us and who He says we are in Him.

SUMMARY

1. Often in the journey to become a powerful leader, we will walk through all kinds of painful experiences that test and shape our character.

2. There are three core areas of powerlessness that God will lead us to overcome as He transforms us into powerful leaders: inadequacy, fear of punishment, and insignificance.

3. It is normal for insecurity to appear as God continues to lead us into places outside our comfort zone and past our limitations.

4. Areas of inadequacy are not causes for condemnation and shame, but places where we are invited to embark on a learning journey, trusting that God will makes us adequate for what He has called us to.

5. In order to be powerful leaders, we have to confront any place where we default to the fear of what other people may think.

6. Those who live out of the lie of insignificance will attempt to build success in their own strength to fulfill the desire they have for greatness.

7. Those who are secure in their identity and worth serve others, while those striving for significance serve themselves.

ACTIVATION

INADEQUACY

1. Take a moment to consider whether there any areas you are struggling with a sense of inadequacy. Ask Jesus, "Is there any place You want to reveal to me where I am operating out of performance or control?"

2. If anything comes to mind, take a moment to repent. "Jesus, forgive me for every area where I haven't trusted You. Forgive me for every way that I have tried to operate out of my own strength rather than accessing Yours. Forgive me for every way I have tried to control the outcome."

3. Then release the feelings of inadequacy to Him, as well as any places of control. "Jesus, I release to You my insecurity about _____. Jesus, I hand control over to You in _____ and I make the choice to trust You."

4. Then ask, "Jesus, what is Your promise to me in this area as I commit to trusting You? What are some specific ways I can step into greater trust in You right now?"

5. Write down the promise and commit to reviewing it on a daily basis as an active reminder to make the choice to trust.

FEAR OF PUNISHMENT

1. Take a moment to search your heart, asking yourself, "Is there a place in my life I am living in fear of what other people may think?" Ask Jesus to reveal if there is anything in this area that He wants to show you.

2. If a place of fear is revealed, ask Jesus, "Can You show me the first time I took on this fear?"

3. Often, a memory will come to mind of a scary or painful situation with another person. With this in mind, ask Jesus, "Is there anyone I need to forgive in this situation?" If so, begin to release forgiveness out loud: "Jesus, I forgive this person for _____." Continue to speak out forgiveness until you have released them from the pain and suffering you experienced through your encounter with them.

4. Then ask, "Jesus, are there any lies I have believed as a result of that situation?"

5. As any lie is revealed, declare out loud, "Jesus, I renounce the lie that _____ and I break agreement with it. What is the truth You want to tell me in its place?"

6. As any lies/truth are revealed, write them down. Actively commit to continuing to review the new truths daily in order to retrain your mind out of the old, subconscious belief system and into the truth that has been revealed.

7. Ask Jesus to show you specific steps you can take in your current circumstances to receive and live out of His supernatural peace and freedom from punishment.

INSIGNIFICANCE

1. Close your eyes and take a moment to calm your mind into a relaxed and peaceful state.

2. Search your heart and ask yourself, "Do I have a desire for significance?" Often, we have not acknowledged that desire to ourselves because it has felt wrong or prideful.

3. Then ask Jesus, "Are there any places I have been looking for significance in external things?" If you get the sense the answer is "Yes," begin to ask where. "What are the things I have been using to prove my worth?"

4. As things come to mind, picture yourself laying them down at the feet of Jesus as you repent. "Jesus, forgive me for using this to build my significance." Then say, "Jesus, I give You all these things I have used to build my own greatness. As I hand them to You, what do You have for me in return?"

5. Then begin to ask Jesus, "How am I significant to You? What do You say about me? What is the greatness that is on my life?'

6. Take the time to soak in the answers, let them impact your heart, and write them down.

7. Make it a daily practice to go back to that place with Jesus, reviewing the truth or allowing Him to speak it freshly to your heart. Build the reservoir of truth that will train your mind and your heart to embrace your identity as His child.

8. Ask Jesus to show you specific ways you can start to live out the truth of your significance in your current circumstances.

5

INSTALLING A LENS OF HONOR

Early in our journey of rebuilding the foundations of the church, Dennis, Marla, and I invited a consultant to come and help us identify the vision, mission, and core values of our church. Over six months, we worked to examine and articulate what was deep in our hearts to accomplish. We weren't looking for catchy words on a piece of paper—we wanted to formulate unchanging statements that would define our organization for years to come. The process was truly valuable in creating unity within our team, and we emerged from it full of the excitement of knowing who we were, where we were going, and how we would behave along the way.

Here are the final statements we agreed upon:

NORTHGATE ALASKA's VISION

Northgate exists to see every heart healed, every family made whole, and every nation transformed by the love of the Father!

NORTHGATE ALASKA's MISSION

To build a family who pursues the presence of God and impacts people by creating places for relationship, healing, and equipping.

OUR CORE VALUES

His Presence

We zealously pursue God and His presence for relationship and purpose. We pray, read His Word, worship, fellowship, and walk in obedience to the Holy Spirit.

Supernatural Lifestyle

We partner with the Holy Spirit to be transformed and to demonstrate the kingdom of God through divine wisdom, spiritual gifts, miracles, signs, and wonders.

The Gospel

We emphasize and proclaim the Love of the Father in sending His Son as a sacrifice for all man's sins. We are ambassadors of the reconciling truth of God and are carriers of this Good News wherever we go.

Healthy Relationships

We sacrificially invest in life-giving relationships in both our natural and spiritual families. We honor people by seeing them as God created them to be and cultivate heart connection through clear communication, understanding, and vulnerability.

Wholeness

We encounter God for the healing of our hearts and the revelation of our identity as sons and daughters. We actively partner with the will of God to heal the spirit, soul, and body of all people.

Greatness

We choose to celebrate, equip, and release every person into
their unique greatness. We empower each person to grow
and flourish in their gifting and calling so that they serve
God and man with excellence.

As you can see, most of this statement is dedicated to articulating our core values. While vision establishes where we are going and mission clarifies how we are going to get there, it is core values that define our behavior and create the cultural boundary lines around what we expect from ourselves and one another in the pursuit of success.

Throughout the process of pursuing clarity around our core values and expected behavior, we were keenly aware that our job as leaders was bring that clarity to our staff team, who in turn would bring it to our volunteers and congregation. We also understood that we had to be able to do this on two levels—communication and demonstration. Unlike vision, core values are not aspirational. If I have a core value of integrity, I do not aspire to have integrity—I consistently display it in my behavior. This is not to say that leaders must be flawless, but it does mean we should have a track record of living up to our values and making swift course corrections when we recognize that our behavior is out of line with what we profess to value. This track record is what positions us to build trust, influence, and alignment with those we are leading and create momentum in shaping the culture.

While all six of the core values we included in our statement were equally important to us, we knew we had reached this point in the history of our church because we needed to close the gap between what we had been preaching for years about having a relational culture of honor and our actual relational behaviors. If we as a leadership team couldn't be successful in demonstrating what healthy relationships were supposed to look like to our staff and congregation, then our ability to move forward in any direction would be compromised.

In particular, as we state in the second sentence in our core value statement on healthy relationships, there were two primary areas of behavior we were committed to teaching and demonstrating: honor and cultivating connection. As the years have unfolded since making this statement, we have discovered much about what it means to lead in practicing these consistently. In this chapter, I'll unpack what we've learned about the first half of the sentence: "We honor people by seeing them as God created them to be . . ." In the following two chapters, we'll explore what it means to "cultivate heart connection through clear communication, understanding, and vulnerability."

BELIEVING IS SEEING

It's easy to think of "seeing" as a passive rather than an active behavior. But seeing people the way God created them to be is anything but passive. We live in a fallen world, where no one yet lives in the fullness of who God created them to be. We all come into the kingdom of God with a belief system that has been shaped by life in this distorted reality, and we see ourselves and others through the lens of this belief system. Only by building a new belief system can we change the way we see. This requires actively renewing our minds with revealed truth and stepping out on that truth with consistent action. Only when we perceive people this way will we treat them with honor, like God does.

Here are some of the core beliefs we have worked to clarify for our team that make up what it means for us to "see people as God created them to be":

- Every person is created in the image of God and is a target for His love.

- The goal of our Christian walk is to love others with the same selfless love God has for us.

- Our ability to love others is the fruit of a relationship with the Holy Spirit.

- We will love people to the level that we are able to see the truth about their value as a son or daughter of God.

- Often we struggle to see the value God places on others because of a lack of understanding for how God sees us.

- The value of any person is separate from their behavior. A renewed mind sees each person's God-given value and does not hold someone's sins against them.

- The way I treat others reveals my thoughts towards them and my beliefs about them.

- Any time pressure comes on me and I react in a way that is inconsistent with the goal of love and honor, it exposes an incorrect belief system within my own heart.

- My job is to manage what is happening inside of me and to see that nothing is allowed to poison my thoughts, feelings, or attitudes towards someone else.

Unraveling the strongholds of ungodly beliefs about people takes time. We all have a lifetime of training in human cultures built upon values that don't align with God's value for people. For example, I grew up in New Zealand, a country that struggles with tall poppy syndrome. Tall poppy syndrome is a social dynamic based on jealousy and false humility. It assumes that those who have achieved success, status, wealth, or prominence need to be cut back down to size, and that everyone should stay conscious of their areas of weakness in order to prevent them from becoming arrogant or overly ambitious. Culturally, the humor in New Zealand is heavily sarcastic and mocking, a type of humor that looks for the weaknesses and mistakes of others and then uses it to get a laugh at that person's expense. A family of a close friend had a sign hanging in their home that summed the mentality up well: "If you are mocked, you are loved." From a young age, I was trained by the culture to see the weaknesses in people and to know them with a negative mindset. I was also trained to believe that it was acceptable to expose and mock the weaknesses of others, especially those I whom loved or those who have achieved success. When you have been trained to see people with a negative mindset like this, it takes time and intentionality to learn to see through the lens of honor.

As leaders, we need to be powerful in seeing ourselves and others through a lens of honor. Classically, there are three basic scenarios where other people's behavior can tempt us to lose sight of who they were created to be and turn our honor off toward them:

1. Behavior that scares us because it raises suspicions
2. Behavior that scares us because it's so different than what we would do
3. Behavior that scares and hurts us because it is legitimately offensive

We are all going to encounter this kind of behavior regularly. We must learn to recognize when we're having an experience where fear and pain are urging us to change our beliefs about people and treat them differently than God does, and make the powerful choice to hold on to His perspective no matter what.

OVERCOMING SUSPICION

Some time ago, I started noticing that a close friend was behaving strangely around me. She wouldn't make eye contact with me at church, and when we did have an interaction, it felt awkward and distant. After it happened more than one time, it seemed obvious to me that there was some kind of disconnection between us.

I started to speculate what the reason for this disconnect could be. I felt sure that I had done something to upset her, and concluded that she had to be walking in offense. I became upset that she would be offended at me without even telling me. I started to feel like she was a bad friend whom I couldn't trust, and was even wondering if our friendship should continue if she was willing to behave that way.

Eventually, I decided to go talk to her. By this point, I already had some strong conclusions as to what her problem was and what would have to change for us to move forward. However, my commitment to practicing healthy confrontation led me to start the conversation with some investigative questions rather than launching in with my opinions.

"It seems you are upset at me, but I have no idea why," I told her. "Can you tell me what is going on?"

As she shared her heart with me, I quickly discovered that my interpretation of her behavior and the conclusions I had reached about it were completely wrong. She had avoided eye contact with me twice and we had one awkward interaction. Those were the facts. The truth was that there could have been many reasons for her behavior, many of which were benign and had nothing to do with me. But I had filled in the rest of the story with a negative assumption that made her the offender and me the innocent victim, which caused me to want to withdraw and self-protect. Every conclusion I had made about her felt logical and true—until I asked for more information.

As I searched my heart to get to the bottom of why I had believed the worst of my friend, I recognized that when I experienced unusual behavior from her, it scared me, and I had allowed that fear to influence my beliefs about her and our relationship. Fear runs only one script in our minds—"You need to protect yourself from this threat!" Whenever we read someone else's behavior as threatening, we are naturally going to see them in a negative light and position ourselves defensively toward them. Instead of moving towards them to find out what's really going on and lean into connection, we start to create distance with them. We start to attribute bad motives to them, and then interpret their other behavior with that assumption, looking for evidence to back up the case we are building to support our belief. Before we know it, we end up convinced that our belief about the other person is true, and feel justified in our self-protective behavior, never recognizing that 1) it's quite possible that our belief is completely false, and 2) even if the person is a genuine threat, no behavior ever gives us permission to turn our honor off toward them.

Again, fear is the motivator for all powerless thinking and behavior, and the enemy of healthy relationships. We must keep watch over our own hearts and refuse to allow fear to shape our beliefs and behavior. We must maintain a healthy self-awareness that recognizes when we are being tempted to frame someone's behavior in a negative light, and commit to being slow to judge and quick to seek truth from the other person. Any time we catch ourselves thinking of someone as a problem, we must be purposeful to retrain ourselves to see their worth and to focus on what is good and worthy of praise. In that way, we turn every experience with potentially scary behavior into opportunities to grow in our love.

OVERCOMING FEAR OF DIFFERENCE

Early in my coaching relationship with Tony, he had me do the Myer-Briggs assessment to help me learn more about the strengths and weaknesses of my personality (ENFJ). One of the statements in my personality profile was this:

> One of their biggest difficulties derives from one of their greatest strengths. While very accomplished at working with other people and groups, they can become depressed, wounded, even bitter if their ideas are met with resistance. They take conflict or rejection very personally, and often carry a grudge against the individuals or groups involved. Disagreements tend to escalate into win-lose issues and become personalized, with loyalties sharply marked, even when the other side had only intended to raise some valid questions.[1]

When I read this at first, I confess that I didn't immediately see how this described my behavior. But, as so often happens when you learn

---

[1] Otto Kroeger and Janet M. Thuesen, *Type Talk: The 16 Personality Types That Determine How We Live, Love, and Work* (New York, NY: Dell Publishing, 1989), 273.

something new, I soon had an experience that showed me just how accurate this statement was about me!

This discovery unfolded after someone on our team came to me for advice about a situation in her personal life. She had overcommitted herself, and now had competing demands on her time. In trying to do everything, she realized that she wasn't doing anything well and was struggling with guilt, particularly that she was letting her family down. She often was not available for them when they wanted to connect.

As we discussed her priorities, she had a clear sense of what they were, with family being very high on the list. We then listed out how her time was being spent and compared that to her priority list. It was clear that her choices were completely inconsistent with her priorities, which was driving the guilt. She wasn't doing the things that were most important to her. She realized she was going to have to make some significant changes in her commitments for her time choices to reflect her priorities. I left the meeting feeling great about what I had helped her discover and confident that it was going to change her life.

However, over time, I noticed she wasn't implementing any of the changes we had discussed. Even as she cleared up some of her earlier commitments, she would just make new ones. She couldn't seem to say "no" to anyone who asked her to be a part of something. I noticed the strain on her family connections was increasing and her friendships seemed to be declining.

The more I observed, the more frustrated I became. I was frustrated that she wasn't taking advice, frustrated because there was a better way to live, and frustrated because I thought she was being foolish in her choices. Frustration often comes from our inability to give grace to others in their imperfections. Over time, my frustration built to anger. I started playing out an imaginary conversation with her where I shared exactly what I thought.

I just had decided to go and have that conversation with her when Tony called me out on my frustration during a coaching call.

"Is your frustration connected to losing something, or is it connected to your own sense of justice and integrity?" Tony asked.

"I am not really losing anything personally, so it must be connected to my sense of justice and integrity. There is just a better way than what she is living right now," I replied.

"Okay, so that answer is your indictor. When your frustration is connected to losing something, it is usually an indication that there is a problem in the relationship and you need to talk to her about how she is affecting you. When your frustration is connected to your own sense of justice and integrity, it indicates that the problem is most likely inside your own heart. It seems that you have a set of expectations on how she should live and if she doesn't meet your expectations you get frustrated. Does that sound right?"

"Yes! It sounds exactly right!"

"And when you get frustrated, you protect your heart by withdrawing from the relationship?"

"Yes! I have been doing that!" I admitted.

Tony began to prompt me to ask Jesus some questions.

"Jesus, what is it that I have expected of her?"

I realized I had been expecting her to live "right" according to my definition of what that was. Essentially, I wanted her to be like me, to live how I would live, and I was judging her because she was so different—her personality type was almost the opposite of mine. I thought I could do a better job of living her life than she was!

"Jesus, what do You see when You look at her?"

Immediately, I saw a scene of the two of us standing next to each other coloring a picture. My picture was very orderly—everything was colored inside the lines. Her picture was covered in splashes of color and squiggles—nothing was inside the lines. Yet I felt His pleasure over each of us and what we were producing. I realized that my strength was to stand back and see the big picture, make a plan, and follow the plan. Her strength was to see the person right in front of her, and, with a pure instinct to help, give them all her attention and affection. I also realized that we needed each other! She needed my strength to help her develop strategy and stay accountable to that strategy so she didn't lose sight of her family as she was captured by the needs around her. I needed her strength to make sure I didn't lose sight of the needs of those right in front of me while I was following the plan.

I learned a lesson that day that has marked me ever since. *When I expected her to be like me, not only did I miss her gift—I sabotaged my own.* Instead of encouraging her and coming alongside to strengthen her from a place of hope and faith, I withdrew from her out of frustration. Instead of receiving her differences as a gift to learn from, I devalued them and rejected her. I could have done serious damage to our relationship if Tony hadn't helped me see what I was doing—turning "the way I do things" into an expectation for her, judging her as being "wrong" for not meeting that expectation, and then reacting by creating distance from her.

I began to practice thanking God for her whenever she came to my mind, celebrating the unique gifts that He had put in her life and the gift she was to me personally. I continued to do this until it reframed the way I thought about her, and when I saw her, there was genuine appreciation for who she was. When we did have a conversation, I went with love and value for her as a person instead of anger and frustration at her choices. Our exchange was transformational and strengthening to our relationship.

Now, while my initial reaction to this woman was influenced by my specific personality type, it's also true that we all tend to struggle learning to relate around our differences with other people. So many of the behaviors we encounter aren't right or wrong, bad or good—they are simply different. Yet we naturally project our "normal" on to other people and feel uncomfortable when they deviate from it. Why? Because we equate sameness with safety. If we think someone is like us, then we feel we can trust them. When they're not like us, it can trigger a deep-seated fear that they won't understand us, meet our needs, or allow us to influence them in a relationship. Like all other relational fears, this fear of difference never leads us toward anything honoring or relationally healthy. Through eyes of honor, we recognize that our differences are designed to enrich and strengthen our lives and relationships—if we seek to understand them, celebrate them, and receive them.

OVERCOMING OFFENSE

Not too long ago, a person I cared about did something that really upset me. Without consulting me, he had made a decision that had set things in motion that would directly impact me negatively, and there was no undoing it. I found out what was happening from someone else. It wasn't the first time he had done something like this. I was disappointed and really frustrated.

Without stopping to think about it, I began venting my frustration to a couple of other people. Eventually, we reached a point in the conversation where we were no longer just talking about what he had done—we were talking negatively about him as a person. I was concluding that he was arrogant and selfish, uncaring about how he affected those around him. In my frustration, I had judged the motives of his heart and was sharing it as if it was fact.

Then, out of nowhere, a question dropped into my spirit and caught me completely off guard: *"Will you oppose and expose him, or will you position yourself on his behalf for breakthrough?"*

Instantly, I felt completely humbled and convicted. I had reacted so quickly in judgment towards him. I felt completely righteous in my indignation—even as I was now sinning against him. I was so focused on his wrong that I did not see my own. Instead of moving toward him in love and positioning myself to fight for his good, I had set myself up to oppose him. Immediately, and somewhat sheepishly, I apologized to the others for what I had just done, shifted the tone of the conversation, and then withdrew to spend some time with God. Something very unsettling had just been revealed in me and I needed to take some time to examine my heart.

As I sought the Lord and asked Him to reveal what He wanted me to learn through this situation, I was reminded of Jesus' words to His disciples in Matthew 24:12: ". . . because lawlessness will abound, the love of many will grow cold" (NKJV). The idea of "growing cold" is the picture of a slow cooling off over time, like putting something hot in the refrigerator. Jesus is not talking here about the love of the world growing cold, but the love of His followers—those who claim to believe in Him, for whom love is the true mark of belonging to Him (John 13:35). There is a warning implicit in this verse. When lawlessness, or sin, is increasing around me, it creates a threat to my love. Lawlessness is the contempt and violation of the law of God—when people turn away from following God's ways and choose things that violate His principles. We are surrounded by lawlessness at different levels—globally, nationally, locally, and also on a personal level in our families and friendships. We see it in the government, in media, in the entertainment industry, and all around us in our churches, workplaces, and homes. Lawlessness is scary, painful, and offensive. It is also creates a very deceptive trap (The Greek word for *offense* means "a trap" and "a stumbling block"[2]) by tempting us to react to sin by sinning ourselves. We feel justified and righteous when we get angry, offended, mistrustful, accusing, controlling, judgmental, punishing, or pessimistic about others' poor choices. We take to social media to vent our opinions about those we oppose. We share our judgments with others and move into gossip and slander. Or we simply hold negative judgements and withdraw from others in our hearts. And the whole time we are doing this, we fail to recognize that we are sinning by turning our love off and allowing it to grow cold.

When we fall for the trap of offense, we are embracing the belief system that people who sin must be judged and punished. We are seeing them through a lens that is completely opposed to the way the Father sees them. His response to a world caught in lawlessness was not to send a punisher, but a Savior—His own Son. His sacrificial love has become the standard for everyone—we are to "walk in love, as Christ also

---

[2] "G4625 - *skandalon* – Strong's Greek Lexicon (KJV)." Blue Letter Bible. Accessed October 15, 2018. https://www.blueletterbible.org//lang/lexicon/lexicon.cfm?Strongs=G4625&t=KJV

has loved us and given Himself for us."[3] One of my favorite definitions of the Greek word for love in this verse, *agape*, is "the kind of love that is always contending for the highest possible good in every situation and is relentlessly contending until it is a present tense reality."[4] The emphasis of this kind of love is completely on the giver, not the receiver. It is offered freely and unconditionally on the basis of the giver's choice, not the receiver's.

1 Corinthians 13:5 says, "Love . . . is not provoked" (NJKV). This means that even in the face of sin or poor judgment, I remain in control of my love, committed to the highest good of the other person, and I refuse to be drawn into a flesh reaction. Even when my heart is under threat, love will not return evil for evil. Love returns only good. If the poor choice of another can provoke a flesh response out of me, then it reveals a problem in my own heart, a place where I need to grow in my love.

One of the most critical things we must remember as leaders is that when we lose the ability to see the truth over a person, we also lose the ability to influence them with our love. The truth of who they are must be held higher than their own behavior, and above our emotions, hurt, or perceptions of a situation. Yes, my friend made a decision that I disagreed with, a decision that hurt and felt arrogant and selfish. But there were deeper truths that needed to govern the way I saw him if I wanted to be able to honor him and respond to the hurt and disagreement in a way that created the opportunity for repair in our relationship.

First, there was the truth that my responsibility toward every offense is to move toward the person with love and forgiveness. It is never to determine motive, assign guilt, or mete out punishment. Second, there was the truth that even if the motives behind his behavior were arrogant and selfish, it wouldn't help anything to turn these into labels for who he was. When my pain and fear had calmed down enough for me to articulate the outcome I truly hoped for in this situation, it was that

---

[3] Ephesians 5:2 NKJV

[4] Kevin Weaver, *Re_Orient: You'll See an Uprising* (It's Feasible, LLC, 2014), 12.

I would be able to let him know how his decision had affected me and ask him to clean up his mess. And in order to do that with any kind of hope, I needed to trust that he wasn't actually a hopelessly arrogant and selfish person, but a powerful person who cared about our relationship and the effect he was having on me.

After I dealt with my heart towards this man, the next step I took was to get more information about his decision. I discovered there were factors I had been unaware of that played into his decision-making process, and that he was under pressure of different expectations from different people. Learning this helped me understand his decision, even if I didn't agree with it and felt sad because it revealed that his priorities were different than what I wanted them to be. Ultimately, the best thing I could do to honor him and protect connection was to adjust my expectations and continue to pursue better communication with him in the future.

HELPING OTHERS SEE

As we become powerful in being able to see people as God created them to be no matter what, we begin to understand that we are positioned to help others see themselves and others through the same lens of honor. Where before we reacted in defensiveness to people's behavior, now we live offensively, showing them the love, delight, patience, and trust of the Father. Ephesians 4:29 instructs us, "Let no unwholesome word proceed from your mouth, but only such a word as is good for edification according to the need of the moment, that it may give grace to those who hear" (NASB). We have the opportunity to be a people who encourage, build up, and promote growth in others, especially in moments of need. Most people aren't having a moment of need when everything is going well. When people are struggling, falling short, or trapped in cycles of bad behavior, they need a word that releases grace—the favor and empowerment of heaven—and invites breakthrough. I have heard it described that our words of edification create a target on the lives of others that attracts heaven to land. We know that we have retrained ourselves to see with heaven's perspective when someone makes a poor choice and we see them as a target for a word of encouragement that brings grace. We start asking, "God, what is it that You are saying over them right now? What is it that they need from You?" After we receive His heart for them in their current situation, and we move to honor them in such a way that brings about their highest good.

SUMMARY

1. Seeing people the way God created them is an active pursuit that requires renewing our minds with truth.

2. It takes time and intentionality to learn to see others with the lens of honor.

3. There are three basic scenarios where other people's behavior can tempt us to lose sight of who they are created to be and turn off our honor towards them:

   a. Behavior that scares us because it raises suspicions

   b. Behavior that scares us because it is different than what we would do

   c. Behavior that scares and hurts us because it is legitimately offensive

4. Offense creates a deceptive trap by tempting us to react to sin by sinning ourselves.

5. No behavior ever gives us permission to turn our honor off towards another person.

6. We must learn to recognize when we are having an

experience where fear or pain are urging us to change our beliefs about others.

7. When we lose the ability to see the truth over a person, we lose the ability to influence them with our love.

ACTIVATION

1. Is there someone with whom you are struggling right now? Someone who is making choices you disagree with? Ask Jesus if there is someone towards whom you have a negative mindset.

2. Take a moment and identify how you are feeling as a result of their behavior. Disappointed? Hurt? Grieved?

3. Start bringing that emotion to Jesus. "Jesus, as a result of their behavior, I am feeling _____." Choose to pour it all out at His feet.

4. Ask "Jesus, is there any place I am holding unfair expectations towards them?" If anything comes to mind, release that expectation back to Him. "Jesus, I release _____ from my expectation to _____. What are Your expectations towards them?"

5. Then ask, "Jesus, how do You see them? What are the things You delight in over them? What are the unique gifts on their life that I could learn from?" Take the time to declare thankfulness over whatever comes to mind.

6. Start a daily practice of thanksgiving over them and declaring what is good about them until you have retrained yourself to celebrate who they are.

7. Ask "Jesus, is there a word of edification that I could bring to them in this season that would release the grace

of heaven?" Start to listen for a word and be prepared to go and encourage them with that word.

8. We encourage you to proactively do steps 5-7 regularly over every person on your team while you are in good relationship, so that when struggles come you have already trained yourself to see the gift they are to you and positioned yourself as an encourager in their life.

6

EXCHANGING THE TRUTH

The second part of our core value for healthy relationships states, "We... cultivate heart connection through clear communication, understanding, and vulnerability." As a team, we strongly agreed that connection thrives or dies according to the quality of our communication. Powerful communication requires the vulnerable exchange of truth with the goal of understanding. Only by exposing our hearts—our thoughts, feelings, and needs—can we connect heart to heart, meet one another's needs, and collaborate effectively in our relationships.

We also understood that one of our specific responsibilities as leaders in the body of Christ was to equip people to "speak the truth in love."[1] The context for this verse is Paul's statement on what we call the fivefold ministry roles of apostle, prophet, evangelist, pastor, and teacher and their function to equip the saints for ministry and maturity. His implication is that "speaking the truth in love" is one of the primary vehicles for and expressions of us growing into mature Christlikeness, and that equipping people in the body of Christ to speak the truth in love is one of leadership's primary responsibilities.

As a leadership team, we certainly wanted speaking the truth in love to be the standard for our communication. However, the more we

---

[1] See Ephesians 4:15.

intentionally pursued this standard, the more realized 1) how much we needed to grow in learning to do this well, and 2) how many bad examples of communication we had been exposed to that we needed to unlearn. More often than not, the communication styles and culture we had experienced and participated in as members and leaders in the church fell short of the biblical standard because they were powerless and fear-driven. As Danny says in *Keep Your Love On*, "Fear is the great hijacker of communication . . . Powerless people communicate out of the fear of truth."[2] When we're afraid of the truth, we either end up speaking truth without love (this is often aggressive or passive-aggressive communication), or we don't speak the truth in the name of love (passive communication). Both hurt our ability to form healthy heart connections.

Truth spoken without love was what I saw most often in the church I attended growing up. The leaders ascribed to a form of church discipline that publicly exposed bad behavior and used shame to coerce and intimidate people into good behavior. I still have a clear memory of the day a church meeting was called because a good friend of our family, then thirteen years old, became pregnant. I remember her shrinking back into the corner as the leaders announced her sin and the other church members surrounded and hugged her parents, weeping with them. The girl was ostracized by many in the church from that moment forward, particularly by those in the youth group, who were learning what was modeled—you must behave to belong. Ultimately, she was driven away from God and the community—as were many others over the years who received the same treatment. Those who remained in the community learned that the truth was not safe there. They performed correctly in public and hid places where they were struggling, rather than going to one another for the support and encouragement they needed for breakthrough.

While publically calling out people's sin wasn't normal in our church culture at Northgate, I did witness instances of truth spoken without

---

[2] Danny Silk, *Keep Your Love On* (El Dorado Hills, CA: Loving on Purpose, 2014), 81-82.

love over the years that were more emotionally driven. Typically, these occurred because someone had been silently tolerating another person's hurtful behavior over long periods of time and allowing resentment to grow until they finally snapped. They started airing their grievances to others, exposing the person and damaging their reputation, or they directly attacked the person with a laundry list of offenses stored up against them. It was obvious that their goal in speaking up was not to repair the relationship, but to lash out in punishment and revenge.

What *was* normal in our church culture, however, was people keeping silent about the truth in the name of being loving, when really they were motivated by fear—either fear of backlash from the person they should be confronting, or fear of hurting the person out of misguided compassion. In my observation and experience, it's very easy for Christian leaders to fall into this false compassion. When we know someone's story and gain compassion for their places of brokenness, we more easily excuse and tolerate their poor choices. What feels like love is actually enabling patterns of bad behavior.

CHOOSING TO PURSUE THE TRUTH

As we began to pursue greater relational health as a leadership team, we soon found ourselves in a situation that required us to choose whether we would continue to allow this pattern of passivity and false compassion in our leadership style or learn to break out of it.

One of our leaders was navigating a very difficult personal struggle and his home life was in chaos. We all knew what was happening, and were praying for breakthrough as he pursued help. At the same time, we were all dealing with the way this stressful situation was "leaking" on to our whole team through his behavior. He was showing up to work and meetings with a very negative attitude—often, the atmosphere would shift as soon as he entered the room. He got offended easily, shut down, snapped at people, and would even get up and walk out of the room in the middle of a conversation. We started to hear reports that this kind of behavior was affecting more than just our staff team, and that his ministry was suffering. We began to dread any interaction with him, yet continued to put off confronting him because we understood why he was behaving so poorly.

Finally, in desperation, we turned to Danny for advice. His initial observation was this: "The history of this place is that, in the name of compassion, you host disease."

There was the truth, spoken in love. For so many years, in relationship after relationship, we had used our compassion for people's circumstances as an excuse not to confront bad behavior, and we were doing it again. Aware that this leader was hurting, we did not want to cause further pain by telling him the truth about how he was affecting us. On the surface, it seemed loving and felt like the godly thing to do. Yet as we discussed it further with Danny, we discovered it was a decision that was actually dominated by fear. We were afraid that if we confronted him while he was struggling so much, he wouldn't take it well, and it would create a big mess on our leadership team.

However, we recognized that continuing to leave the situation unaddressed would also create a mess. This leader would remain completely unaware that his behavior was systematically destroying his relationships and reputation with everyone around him. We would also send the message to everyone on our team and organization, "If you are experiencing pain in your life, it is okay for you to behave badly around us." We were allowing "disease"—toxic, anxiety-producing behavior that was very harmful both to him and to us. This was not love and was the opposite of the culture we wanted to build—a culture where people were expected and encouraged to walk in wholeness, even in the middle of difficult circumstances.

Gradually, we started to present this leader with some feedback about his behavior, starting with what we deemed the most minor issues. Unfortunately, as we had feared, he did not respond to it well, choosing instead to take offense at the feedback. That escalated into bigger discussions where he totally refused feedback, and even threw a tantrum complete with yelling, storming out, and slamming doors. Though he later apologized for that behavior, he persisted in refusing to listen and adjust as we were asking him to do. Eventually, we had to have a "This isn't working" conversation where we explained that he didn't have the capacity to lead on our team and we needed to remove him.

This whole experience was quite difficult and painful, yet in many ways, it represented a significant and necessary step of growth in our pursuit of a healthy standard of communication on our team. We wanted to be a team and a church that refused to allow fear of the truth to infect our relationships and were committed to passionately pursue the truth without fear, understanding that this was the only way to foster genuine connection and a culture of healthy relationships. As we moved forward from our experience with this leader, we agreed that we needed to make it a primary objective to establish a high value for and practice of exchanging feedback on our team.

OVERCOMING FEAR OF FEEDBACK

Painful experiences with feedback seem to be a universal human experience, which means we all have fear triggers (defensive reactions) to overcome if we want to grow in giving and receiving feedback in relationships. If you're wondering whether you have any defensive reactions to feedback, here are some classic behaviors to check for:

1. You can't remember the last time someone gave you feedback.

2. You have a negative expectation any time someone unexpectedly asks to talk to you. You find yourself wondering what you have done wrong.

3. You immediately make excuses or move to explain yourself.

4. You immediately disagree with them or debate their perspective.

5. You shift blame onto someone else.

6. You use your position of authority to silence the other person.

7. You start feeling critical of the person who is attempting to talk to you.

8. You use your emotions to stop the conversation with statements like, "That hurts my feelings."

9. You take offense and leave upset at the other person, often going to someone else to present your side of the story.

10. You leave without taking ownership of the behavior that impacted the other person.

When we enter a feedback conversation in a defensive posture, we've already set ourselves up to resist, rather than receive, whatever the other person wants to tell us. When we persist in this defensiveness, it's like we're walking around with a big neon sign that says, "You cannot tell me anything." The people around us get the message that protecting ourselves is more important than learning the truth that will help us protect our relationships.

Having seen firsthand the kind of anxiety and dysfunction that feedback-resistant leaders created on a team, and being soberly aware that we must avoid becoming such leaders ourselves, Dennis, Marla, and I began pursuing action steps that would help us dismantle our own defensive reactions to feedback, learn and practice exchanging feedback, and establish the value for feedback throughout our organizational culture.

For my part, I was very aware that I had some feedback triggers to address. From my earlier experiences in ministry, I had learned that if I was unexpectedly called into a meeting, there was a high chance that it was because I had done something wrong and I was in trouble. As a result, any time I heard things like, "Have you got a minute?" my anxiety would start to escalate. I would head into these conversations reviewing everything I had recently said or done, trying to predict what I was in trouble for, and deciding how I could defend myself from what was inevitably coming.

Two things created a safe place for me to start confronting these triggers and getting comfortable giving and receiving feedback. First, engaging in leadership coaching with Tony not only provided me with excellent feedback for myself—it was also time where I specifically focused on learning how to have effective feedback exchanges in my current relational scenarios on the team. Second, we created an oversight team, which included Danny and Tony, during our restructuring process that provided us with something we had never had before— somewhere we could go outside of ourselves for help if our core values were violated or if we got stuck in a problem with communication and connection.

Creating these safe places for feedback did wonders for helping me lower my anxiety around impromptu feedback conversations, both receiving and giving, that arose in the course of leading. When someone asked me, "Do you have a minute?" I would still feel the old fear come up, but I now had the truth I needed about the safety and commitment from the team to be able to talk myself through it. I would tell myself, "You don't have to be afraid anymore of making a mistake. This is a safe place. The worst that could happen is that you may have a mess you need to clean up." I discovered that most of the time, fear had led me to expect the worst when in the end the conversation wasn't even a confrontation. But I also discovered that when it was a confrontation, I didn't need to be afraid. Receiving feedback kept me humble, helped me to grow, and actually strengthened my relationships. I learned to welcome it rather than be afraid of it.

PULLING OUT FEEDBACK

As leaders, we recognized that we needed to be more intentional and visible in consistently seeking feedback from one another and our team, both to make this habitual for ourselves and to send the message that this was the expected behavior in our culture. Dennis established the habit of periodically checking with me and Marla and asking us directly, "Is there any feedback you have for me that would be helpful for me, that you may not have told me yet?" She and I began to do the same with each other and our direct reports. We introduced exercises during staff meetings that allowed us to debrief and practice giving both encouraging and constructive feedback to the team. For a season, we had everyone on the staff team take a turn leading a staff meeting with some kind of leadership development as the focus. Afterward, they had to seek out specific feedback from a minimum of three people about what they liked and what could be improved. We also set up a review system that included very direct questions facilitating feedback in both directions between senior leadership and staff. With all of these exercises and practices, and in our day-to-day interactions, we leaned into actively encouraging and calling on our team members to contribute feedback, aware that we needed to prove to them that we really wanted it and would make it safe for them to give it.

On one occasion, I facilitated a meeting with a small group of leaders in one of our key ministries. The goal of the meeting was to brainstorm ideas on how we could improve the ministry and grow on the solid platform of what was already happening. In order to grow, however, we had to be willing to change some of the ways we were currently doing things.

As we discussed different ideas, I could tell that one of our leaders at the table was struggling with some of my suggestions. He started to break eye contact and disconnect from some of the conversation. My attempts to draw him out with questions didn't work, and I left the meeting knowing he was not in a good place.

I left the matter for a couple of days, aware that he was a thinker who needed time to process. Then I went in to see him in his office. "I noticed at our meeting that you seemed to be having a hard time with some of the things we were discussing," I said. "What's going on?"

"Nothing!" he replied quickly. "I'm good!"

"Can I tell you something about me?" I asked. "I want you to know that I want the people on this team to tell me what they think and what they see. I don't want them to try and keep me happy and just tell me what I want to hear. You are the person on the ground in this ministry. If you don't tell me what you see, I won't have all the information I need to make a good decision. In your silence, I may make a decision that would ultimately harm what we are trying to build."

He paused, then responded, "But I really want to honor you."

"I think you and I have a different definition of honor!" I said frankly. "It doesn't honor me to just agree with everything I say. It honors me when you trust me enough to tell me what you are thinking and feeling."

Finally, it seemed, I convinced him to trust me. "Well in that case, I do have some questions," he admitted.

"Excellent! I want to hear them!" I encouraged.

As he shared his questions and concerns, he raised some valid points that I had not previously considered. He could see multiple problems with my suggestions, all of which needed to be identified in order to refine our decision-making process. Had I not heard his thoughts, we most likely would have raced ahead, implemented a weak plan, and then had to troubleshoot the problems that he could see coming after they arose.

As he shared, he experienced my willingness to listen and saw that his questions didn't offend me. He also discovered that his suggestions actively changed and shaped the plan for moving ahead. After I thanked him for his honesty, he agreed not to hesitate in the future to share his thoughts and feelings or to ask questions as they arose. A positive experience with giving feedback created the willingness to continue to do it in the future.

RECEIVING FEEDBACK WELL

The ability to receive feedback and turn it into personal and relational growth is a learned behavior. Once we move past our natural defensive reactions, we can train ourselves to respond in a way that makes it easy for people to approach us and celebrates the courage that it takes for people to tell the truth. The more we model a healthy response to feedback, the more safety enters the environment and people begin to choose to walk in the light without being afraid.

Here are the steps we have embraced to receive feedback graciously and put it to work to strengthen our connections:

1. Be approachable.

Stay aware of body language, facial expressions, and eye contact. Closed body language often discourages people from approaching us, while open body language and positive facial expressions (smiles!) encourage them.

2. Listen to understand.

Once we gain control of our natural instinct to defend ourselves, we can choose to actively listen. Active listening means we take the time to absorb what the other person is saying and reflect back what we have heard before we attempt to respond. We do not present our thoughts until we make sure we have accurately understood the message the other person is sending us. Listening well enables us to receive helpful feedback even from people who are presenting it poorly.

When it comes to receiving feedback on our behavior and how someone is experiencing us in a relationship, it's important that we listen for certain pieces of information, namely:

- What is the behavior they're describing?
- What is the emotional experience this behavior is creating for them?
- What do they need to experience from me?
- How are they asking me to adjust?

3. Ask clarifying questions.

Asking clarifying questions is part of active listening. It is an essential tool for letting the other person know how well you understand the message they are sending, and for helping them if they are struggling to deliver that message well. Here are some questions that can help the person clarify their feedback, provide you with the information you need, and assure both of you that you are understanding one another:

- Can you give me an example that illustrates what you are telling me?

- How did you feel when that happened?

- What did you need to feel?

- Is that everything? Is there anything else you need to tell me?

As leaders, we should be prepared to assist and equip people in giving us and other team members feedback—doing so is one of the main ways we demonstrate that we are passionate about learning the truth in order to protect connection. Feedback may come in many forms, from people who are exploding in anger to those who are fearful and unclear. Asking questions will help lower their anxiety and draw out anything of value in what they are trying to communicate.

For example, a close friend once sat me down somewhat nervously and recounted a moment from a social situation we had been in the previous week. She then told me, "I need you to know I felt bullied by you in that moment."

Multiple thoughts raced through my head within seconds. On one hand, I felt respect and admiration rising that she had the courage to come and tell me how she felt. At the same time, defensive thoughts instantly sprang to mind.

Bullied? That seems a bit harsh. No one has ever called me a bully before!

A narrative of self-justification and blame-shifting quickly followed.

I wasn't bullying you in that moment. Anyone could see that we were just having fun. You must be far more sensitive than I thought!

Thankfully, my feedback training went into action and immediately flagged these thoughts as defensive reactions that would block my ability to receive feedback and hurt our relationship. I decided to lay aside the instinct to protect myself and invalidate her feelings, and shift into active listening with the goal of better understanding what she was telling me.

I started with a clarifying question: "At the time, it seemed to me that we were having fun and everyone was laughing. Can you help me understand what wasn't fun for you?"

As we discussed the situation further, she shared some history that I previously had not known about her. In the light of this new information, I could see how some of the ways I had behaved in the social situation were, at the very least, insensitive, and could have felt like bullying. I was horrified! Gaining understanding of how I had impacted her in that moment led me to the desire to immediately clean up my mess.

4. Clean up the mess.

If you did something that you recognize hurt someone else, own the behavior, apologize for how they experienced you and make a verbal commitment to change.

Once I understood how seriously I had affected my friend, I was truly repentant. "Bullied" is a strong emotion, and I never wanted her to feel that powerless or overwhelmed in our relationship. Now that I knew she had experienced me that way, it was important that I fully communicate how I felt in order to restore trust. Sometimes, when there has been a more serious breach in relationship, a simple "Sorry" is inadequate to clean up the mess. Instead, I chose to express the level of my remorse.

"I now recognize that when I questioned you in this area in front of everyone that you felt bullied by me. I see that it was totally inappropriate and hurtful. The fact that I did that to you makes me feel ashamed and horrified. I don't ever want you to experience me that way again, so I commit to being far more sensitive to those kind of situations in the future. I am so sorry. Will you please forgive me?"

My friend responded right away with forgiveness, and we left the conversation both feeling reconnected. Since that exchange, we have often reflected on how navigating that hard situation together actually strengthened our relationship rather than destroying it!

5. Express gratitude.

Thank them for telling you and affirm the courage that it took to move towards you. Take the time to recognize and reinforce that this is exactly the culture you want to build.

6. Filter the feedback.

Understanding the feedback someone is giving you does not mean that you must accept or agree with it as 100% accurate. The person may have interpreted your behavior through their own wounding, life experiences, or judgment of your motives. Take the time to process through what was said, examine your heart, and decide what feedback you will take and adjust for, and what needs to be set aside. It often helps to process feedback with people who know you well and who are trusted to tell you the truth.

7. Consider a follow-up conversation.

If there are points in the feedback that you strongly disagree with, it helps to wait before having further conversation. That gives you the time to get your emotions under control, process what was said, and check the validity of the feedback with someone else before you decide on your response. This allows you to present a different perspective while still demonstrating your willingness to receive and consider any feedback that was given.

CONCLUSION

The more we have been able to create positive and effective exchanges with feedback as a team, the more our value for feedback has grown. Painful memories from the past have been overshadowed by experiencing feedback as some of our greatest fuel for personal and relational growth. As leaders, we have shifted from being nervous to learn about how the people around us are experiencing us to being passionate about doing so, and encouraging everyone in our environment to share this passion. Perhaps most critically, going after a team culture with a high value for feedback has laid the foundation for us to be powerful in having the kinds of conversations that can be most scary and painful in any relationship—conversations that include disagreement or confrontation.

SUMMARY

1. Powerful communication requires the vulnerable exchange of truth with the goal of understanding.

2. When we're afraid of the truth, we either end up speaking truth without love (this is often aggressive or passive-aggressive communication), or we don't speak the truth in the name of love (passive communication). Both hurt our ability to form healthy heart connections.

3. We must guard against withholding the truth and excusing bad behavior out of false compassion.

4. We must become resilient to our defensive reactions to feedback so we can send the message to those around us that we are a safe place ot receive feedback.

5. Leaders must be intentional in seeking and receiving feedback if they want this to be the expected behavior in their team culture.

6. Here is the model we have found effective for receiving feedback well:

    a. Be approachable.

    b. Listen to understand.

    c. Ask clarifying questions.

    d. Clean up the mess.

    e. Express gratitude.

    f. Filter the feedback.

    g. Consider a follow-up conversation.

7

CULTIVATING HEALTHY CONFRONTATION

One morning during our leadership meeting, we ended up in a heated debate. After learning that one of our dearly loved church members had been diagnosed with cancer, Dennis had come to the meeting with a whiteboard and started asking us questions about our Scriptural beliefs on healing and how we were going to position ourselves in prayer. His goal was for us to build faith and agreement to press in for a miracle. However, we quickly discovered that we didn't all agree on our beliefs around healing and a lively discussion ensued. We debated whether it was always God's will to heal and shared our thoughts around the idea of "an appointed time to die."[1]

I had enjoyed the debate and the opportunity to explore different viewpoints, and had left the meeting energized, even though we hadn't all come to an agreement. However, I soon learned that not everyone had had the same experience. A staff member stopped by my office later that day and said, "Carla, you might want to go downstairs. Angela is in the youth office crying."

I quickly headed over to sit down with Angela and ask her what was going on.

---

[1] See Ecclesiastes 3.

"I got home from that meeting and realized I just wanted to quit and run away," she confessed to me. "So I thought I had better come back in and talk to someone."

"I am so glad you came back!" I assured her. "Why did you want to quit?"

"Well, now that you know that I have a different doctrine than you, I thought I better quit before you fire me," she answered.

"Why would we fire you?"

She looked at me, confused. "Because I have a different belief about healing!"

"Angela, we are not going to fire you!" I responded. "We aren't always going to agree on everything. We have been on a journey of discovery in this area over the last ten years where our own beliefs about healing have changed. As long as we can honor one another while we disagree, it's okay that we do!"

I could see the skepticism in her eyes as she sat and looked at me, trying to process what I had just said.

"Angela, has something like that happened to you before?" I asked gently.

"Yes! At our last church. We worked there for a number of years, but when the pastor found out we had a different doctrine about healing than he did, he fired us. When he fired us, he told us that he had never really liked us or enjoyed working with us during our time there. I have just been waiting for that same thing to happen here."

I was astonished that anyone would say something like that to her. In her three years as part of our team she had been a delight to work with, constantly joyful, full of encouragement, and quick to serve.

"Wow, that sounds really hurtful," I said. "Would you be open to inviting Jesus to come and speak into that place?"

With her permission, we began to explore some past places of wounding she had picked up from church leadership. Her experiences had taught her to be afraid and to keep herself protected because people in places of spiritual authority were unpredictable and unsafe. She wrestled to trust as Jesus invited her to take down her walls of self-protection and allow Him to become her protector. As she got breakthrough in releasing her fear and pain to Him, she recognized that she would have to open her heart and begin to build trust with our leadership team. I left our time together impressed that in the midst of such a strong instinct to quit and run, she had pushed past her fear, chosen vulnerability, and was pursuing wholeness.

LEADING WITHOUT PUNISHMENT

I wish I could say that Angela's story of church leadership wounding was uncommon. Over the past three years, partially due to our purposeful development of a safe leadership culture, numerous people have joined our church who were once pastors and leaders at other churches or ministries around the country. Many of them now serve at our church in some capacity, including on our core team. As we have grown in relationship and the pursuit of wholeness, we have heard story after sad story of accusation, division, and broken relationships that have left many with wounds, broken trust, and a fear of authority.

We have also been asked to help a number of people on leadership teams at churches around the world who are wrestling with similar issues. Again and again, we discover that the core problem affecting these teams is an unhealthy leadership model that uses fear, shame, and religious pressure to control those within the organization. In almost all cases, the leaders do not make themselves available for feedback and are not able to be confronted. They shut down people with different opinions through asserting their position of authority, in a military style of leadership. As a result, team members live powerless and afraid, becoming increasingly silenced and wounded in the environment that they are in. Often, they are afraid to speak up out of a distorted belief of what honor looks like in their situation.

In many ways, the stories we have heard from these wounded ministers mirror many of our own experiences. In our approximately twenty years of involvement in churches and missions organizations around the world, my husband and I have had to navigate our own share of hurtful experiences. We have made many mistakes and unwise decisions as we have grown in ministry. We have also been yelled at multiple times, cursed at, threatened, abruptly fired, told that our leader was cutting us out of his life, and confronted with lists of things we had done wrong, some that were over a year old. We have had finances abruptly pulled from our ministry, been told that we couldn't minister to a certain group of people, had false reports said and believed about us, and been accused of many things that made us feel misunderstood and devalued.

In order to become healthy leaders ourselves and lead in building healthy teams and culture, we've had to confront these painful experiences, forgive those who have hurt us, forgive ourselves, and most importantly, identify and lock on to the genuine heart of leadership that we want to carry. All these experiences have taught us who we don't want to be and which goals and practices we don't want to pursue. But reacting to what we don't want is no way to grab on to what we do want. Reacting to what we don't want is a fear-based posture, and the whole problem with dysfuctional leadership in the first place is that it comes from a posture of fear. As long we we stay in fear, we will only reproduce something powerless and dysfunctional.

Unhealthy, powerless leaders are ruled by the fear of punishment. They believe that if they display weakness, make a mistake, or don't have the right answer, their power and position will be taken away. They see people with different opinions, gifts, or strengths as a threat, and acknowledging growth areas and weaknesses as a tactical error. And the culture of fear in their hearts is what they produce around them, displayed most obviously in their style and dynamics of communication. The goal of their communication is always self-protection. This is why they resist feedback, refuse to create space for healthy discussion, debate, and disagreement, and use confrontation and correction to punish and control.

Healthy, powerful, honoring leaders, in contrast, refuse to be ruled by the fear of punishment. They have embraced the truth that God does not punish our weaknesses and mistakes, but rather moves toward us in love to bring repentance, restoration, wisdom, and strength in those areas. Because they have allowed the perfect love of God to overcome the fear of punishment in their hearts,[2] they do not take a self-protective posture, but a posture of self-giving and service to those around them. Their own journey of healing and growth fuels their passion to equip and encourage others along their own journeys toward maturity. They delight in the unique gifts, strengths, and greatness that God has put in each person, and consider it an honor and privilege to call those out and create opportunities for them to be developed. They also fearlessly move toward people to speak truth in love when they see behavior that threatens growth or connection. As they demonstrate that confrontation and correction are totally free of all punishment and control, and have the singular goal of inviting people to become powerful in protecting "us," they create a safe environment for people to risk, fail, clean up their messes, learn, grow, and strengthen relationships.

BUILDING SOMETHING TO PROTECT

As we have pursued this model for our leadership and attracted many people like Angela to our team, we've recognized that our job is to help our team members overcome the influence of powerless leadership in their lives while equipping them to operate as powerful leaders in our environment. It's not enough to communicate that in our culture, feedback, lively debate, accountability, and confrontation are expected, because those very words elicit painful memories of when those things involved criticism, rejection, manipulation, disconnection, and punishment. We have to provide them with opportunities for the same kind of healing we've received, while creating healthy, safe experiences with these types of interactions.

---

[2] See 1 John 4:18.

As I previously mentioned, we have invested time and finances in yearly Sozo ministry for our team. This alone has established the understanding and expectation that every one of us is committed to being on a journey toward wholeness. It has driven away the lie that brokenness is equated with weakness and deserving of mistrust and disconnection. Rather, it has affirmed that being vulnerable about our areas of brokenness is an act of strength that drives away shame and leads to freedom. This is why James instructs us, "Confess your sins to each other and pray for each other that you may be healed."[3] This only works in a healthy, punishment-free culture. One of the signs that a culture is healthy is that people freely confess their areas of struggle to one another, confident that they are surrounded by allies who will champion their breakthrough.

Establishing Sozo ministry in our culture has not only caused every member of our team to experience healing and breakthrough, it has also equipped the team to use Sozo tools on themselves and others. It isn't uncommon to hear the question, "What lie are you believing?" as we help one another get to the bottom of problems that come up. The culture has truly shifted from one where we were hiding our areas of pain and struggle out of fear to one where we address points of pain and partner with others to gain healing and believe truth in the pursuit of a transformed life.

Most importantly, inviting our team to join us on the vulnerable journey of self-discovery, growth, and wholeness has enabled us to form a deeper level of connection than any of us had previously experienced as leaders. This, in turn, has given us something to protect! As we are now experiencing firsthand, protecting connection is always the healthiest motivator for powerful communication. The more connected we've become, the more we've had the courage to move toward each other in moments where we need to make room for one another's feedback or differing opinions, set limits and keep one another accountable, or confront and bring correction.

---

[3] James 5:16 NLT

TRAINING FOR HEALTHY CONFRONTATION

One of our guidelines for powerful communication is that when someone has a conflict or issue with someone else on the team, they go to them directly to confront and resolve it. We do not allow anyone on the team to behave like a victim and take a complaint they have to someone who is not directly part of solving the problem. Whenever someone tries this, we enforce our guideline by asking two simple questions:

1. "Are you going to tell them you have a problem, or am I going to tell them you have a problem?"

2. "When are you going to tell them by?"

As difficult as it feels to create such a strong boundary, every time we have done it, it has resulted in an increase in the sense of safety that surrounds the team. Even the person who experienced the boundary has recognized how safe they feel in an environment where they do not have to feel afraid that people will be upset at them without them knowing.

We have also developed a six-step model that we train everyone on our team to use when they confront someone:

1. Take it to the Lord.

2. Gain perspective.

3. Confront fear.

4. Choose curiosity.

5. Practice vulnerability.

6. Learn from the experience.

TAKE IT TO THE LORD

It's amazing how easy it is, even for us as Christian leaders, to react and make decisions about our course of action before we have engaged with God to receive peace and perspective on the situation. I've done it often enough to know that this is never wisdom. In the presence of strong emotions, our intelligence goes down, our judgment gets clouded, and we are likely to come to conclusions without seeing clearly or correctly. We must avoid making decisions about people when we are not in a place of peace. As we humble ourselves and pour out our emotions to Jesus, it diffuses the intensity of the situation, allows peace and rational thinking to return, and opens our ears to hear Him speak into the situation.

GAIN PERSPECTIVE

We encourage people to ask themselves two questions to gain awareness and understanding of how they are perceiving the issue or situation to be confronted:

- Am I viewing this person through a lens of honor?
- What is my personal responsibility in this situation, given the nature of our relationship and the problem?

Our core value of honoring people by seeing them as God created them to be calls us to always view people from a positive, value-based mindset. If I see a person as a problem or if I have a negative mindset towards them, then I have not yet gained correct perspective. If I have any other goal in speaking the truth than to contend for their highest good, to see them grow and succeed, or to protect our relational connection, then I am not yet operating out of love. It is important to continue to seek God for the truth of how He sees others, until the motivation of our hearts towards them is pure and any sense of vindication has been cleansed.

We also need perspective on ourselves, our relationship with the person, and the situation we're confronting so we can move forward with wisdom. Sometimes gaining perspective will show us that we need to not be passive and confront an issue before it becomes worse. In other scenarios, we may recognize that it is not our reponsibility to tell the person what we see, or that it's not the time to do so.

One of the effects we've seen of creating an empowering culture that encourages people to speak up and confront issues is that some people will become "truth police" where they feel personally responsible for confronting everyone around them with their observations about areas they could improve. They make appointments with pastors and leaders to tell them how they should be doing their jobs, constantly correct the behavior of their friends, and use ministry opportunities to instruct people how to be "better." Often, they are left wondering why people no longer want to be around them! Requiring this step of gaining perspective invites them to manage themselves better so they can be more effective in building trust and safety with people.

CONFRONT FEAR

A while back, a team member came to me for some coaching on how to approach a family member with whom he was having relational struggles. After our initial conversation, I proceeded to check in with him at various intervals to see how the confrontation had gone. Each time I did, however, he had a fresh excuse for why he hadn't yet talked to the person.

"Well, I am going to, but it just doesn't seem like the right time. They are really busy at work right now and just seem really stressed out. I think I should wait until there isn't so much going on in their lives."

After hearing multiple excuses, as well as his report that things were continuing to happen in the relationship that were causing pain and disconnection, I said, "Have you considered that no time is going to feel like a good time to have a hard conversation? That perhaps you are looking for ways to put it off because you are afraid? That you may have to choose courage, push through the fear, and go towards them regardless?"

After considering this, he admitted that he had been operating out of fear. He had been trying to prepare himself emotionally and plan what he was going to say, but as soon as he got in front of the other person, fear came up and he lost courage. Once he saw this, however, he was able to be intentional about pushing through his fear and finally succeeded in confronting the person. There has been breakthrough in the relationship as a result.

As we train new members of our team in the art of healthy confrontation, I have noticed that they almost always back down the first few times. As situations come up, they will come to me for coaching, get mentally and emotionally prepared with all the tools, go into the meeting, and be suddenly hit with a reason not to say something in that moment. I often hear things like, "They were really tired, so it just didn't seem like the right time." The intense anxiety they feel around practicing such a difficult relational tool causes them to generate excuses on behalf of the other person and they go into avoidance. Sometimes, they will make excuse after excuse until the window of appropriate time in which to confront the person after a situation occurred is closed and it is no longer an option.

Going into a conversation where you cannot control the outcome or predict the response of the other person can easily trigger relational fears. "What if they get angry? What if they don't like me? What if this becomes the end of our relationship?" It is impossible to move forward and speak the truth in love when our hearts are dominated by fear. If anxiety starts to creep in, if we find ourselves delaying hard conversations or backing down mid-conversation, it is an indication that fear is present. It is important to deal with the root of the fear to gain the freedom to move forward in love.

CHOOSE CURIOSITY

Curiosity is a posture that says, "Even after I have gone to the Lord for perspective and gained as much awareness of the situation as I can on my own, I still don't know everything that is going on here. So one of the goals in this confrontation is to get more information about what is really happening." Being only one of the people in the relationship means I only know half of the story. I know what I observe, I know the impact that something had on me, and I know my own thoughts and emotions. But I do not know what is happening in the heart or motives of the other person, and I must refuse to become their judge. Approaching a person with curiosity allows for a heart connection and a chance for deeper understanding to shape my perspective. Curiosity starts with questions: "Can you help me understand? What was happening in you in that moment? I noticed _____, can you tell me about that?"

Recently, we hosted a big community event on our church property. Our staff worked hard to do it with excellence, but in the process, there was a lot of stress and tension. I noticed how bad the stress had gotten when one of our usually easygoing staff members nearly bit my head off when I walked in the door one day. Something she was looking for had been moved, and when I told her where it was, she firmly told me off in front of a number of people for not communicating that information to her sooner. I responded with kindness, but left the situation feeling disrespected by the interaction.

After I had time to process my emotions and plan a response, I came back to talk to her. "You seem stressed," I observed. "Can you help me understand what is happening inside of you?"

As she shared, I quickly picked up that she was overwhelmed with the amount of responsibility she had for the event to the point that she wasn't sleeping at night. She needed my help to reallocate some of the tasks on her list. I apologized to her for not noticing sooner, went through the list with her, and handed off some jobs to other staff members. Once we addressed the immediate point of pain, I could see her

117

visibly begin to relax as the stress she had been carrying melted away. By asking her questions, I gained information that I did not have before and was able to meet her immediate needs.

Once the pressure of the immediate need was taken care of, her heart was able to hear my concern about how she was communicating under stress. To introduce this concern, I once again started with a question.

"Are you aware that when you are stressed, your communication style changes?" I asked.

"No! Does it? How?"

From our place of connection, I was able to share with her how I had experienced our interaction, as well as some similar scenarios I had observed. She immediately apologized and made a commitment to clean up some of the other messes that had been made.

This allowed me to create a challenge for her: "What are you going to do to make sure this doesn't happen next time you get stressed?"

With a few more questions and a small amount of feedback from me, she made an excellent plan to gain some tools for dealing with stress. The conversation reached the best possible conclusion through a series of questions that communicated honor and allowed her to be powerful. Not once did I tell her she had a problem, what her problem was, or what she needed to do to fix it. The conversation ended with her thanking me for being honest with her.

PRACTICE VULNERABILITY

The cowardly approach to confrontation is to protect ourselves by making the entire conversation about the other person. We keep our own heart hidden by saying, "Here is what you have done wrong. Let me tell you about you." However, this style of communication leaves no room for connection or curiosity, and often communicates judgment, which is almost always met with resistance. Judgment goes beyond communicating "Here is what you have done" and into a conclusion that states, "This is who you are." For example, "You always leave your dishes in the sink. You are such a messy person." Most people will immediately move to defend themselves from someone who comes at them with a negative statement or conclusion, thereby preventing the conversation from leading to any change, growth, or restoration of connection.

Communicating with vulnerability takes courage, because it means choosing to let the other person see what is happening inside our hearts and minds without doing anything to control their response or the outcome of the conversation. Instead of telling them about them, we invite them to understand us through "I feel" and "I need to feel" statements. This gives them the opportunity to see the impact their choices have made on us and allows them to respond to our heart. It requires us to risk their rejection, but it also means showing them that we trust them to care about our hearts and the effect they're having in the relationship. It is impossible to build trust and healthy relationships without this level of vulnerability.

Recently, I watched one of our young, new leaders on the team lead an excellent meeting for new people who wanted to connect to our church. She had facilitated a setup that had tables of new people mixed in with long-standing members and leaders in the church. During her talk and the subsequent small group discussions, I watched as one of the group leaders texted on his cell phone underneath the table for a long period of time. Even as the group discussion went on, he ignored the people talking around him until finally someone directed a question directly to him. Then I watched him fumble to answer as he clearly was disconnected from the conversation.

Afterwards, I talked to the event leader about how to handle the situation and confront this leader. I encouraged her to identify her feelings, find her "I" statements, and keep it simple. She developed a communication plan that looked something like:

"I noticed that while I was speaking and while the group discussion was going on, you were on your phone underneath the table and you missed a lot of what was happening. That made me feel disrespected in my role, but even more, I felt concerned about what was happening in the discussion around the table without you present as a facilitator. I need to know that I can count on you to be fully present in your assignment. Can you help me understand what was happening with you?"

She later reported to me that she had had a great conversation with this man. He had explained that he had been under a huge amount of stress during the event, and they agreed to let him take some time away from his leadership responsibilities until he could be fully present.

LEARN FROM THE EXPERIENCE

As time has passed and we have practiced the tools of healthy confrontation on our team, we have all had many experiences, both good and bad. I personally have had conversations that have gone exactly according to plan, with a beautiful connection of hearts and a genuine shift in behavior. I have had people come and confront me using the above tools, which gave me the opportunity to repent for actions that had hurt them, resulting in mutual respect and much deeper relationship. I have also had conversations that ended with people yelling at me, storming off, or directly telling me that I was wrong and rejecting anything I had to say.

All of these are opportunities to learn and grow. From the conversations that went well, I review and ask myself:

1. What were the key things that made this conversation successful?

2. What did I do well that I should do again in the future?

3. Are there any places that I could continue to improve, or where I backed away from what I really needed to communicate?

From the conversations that went poorly, I review and ask myself:

1. When did the conversation take a turn for the worse? Can I identify why?

2. Is there anything else I could have done at that point to get the conversation back on track?

3. Are there any ways that I contributed to that not going well?

4. What would I do differently if I could have that conversation again?

5. What is my next step going to be with this person?

While I cannot take responsibility if the other person is simply not open, I have learned and grown in my communication from almost all of the conversations that didn't go well. I have become better prepared to navigate different forms of defensive responses, to adjust my communication style according to personality type, and to say hard things in a way where people thank me and leave feeling loved. That kind of growth can only come through experience—both good and bad!

CONCLUSION

There's no doubt about it—relationships with other human beings can be messy and uncomfortable. And in a way, fostering a culture where people are required to be powerful and honoring brings that reality to the surface in a way that's impossible to ignore. The difference we are seeing on our team, however, is what happens when we as leaders are not afraid of the mess, but instead, lean into it, and encourage those around us to do the same. Again and again, we see people like Angela who, even though their first instinct is to run away from disagreements, conflict, and painful or scary situations, choose to come back and move toward other team members with vulnerable honesty. The result of removing fear from the mess is that resolving the mess, without fail, produces learning, growth, and stronger connections. This, in turn, fuels our hope and courage to risk more in our relationships, pursue the truth fiercely, and love one another with genuine, sacrificial love.

SUMMARY

1. Powerless leaders are ruled by fear of punishment.

2. When we have a culture of fear in our hearts, we will reproduce fear in the world around us.

3. Powerful, honoring leaders embrace the truth that God does not punish our weaknesses and mistakes.

4. We must drive away the lie that brokenness is equated with weakness and deserving of mistrust and disconnection.

5. Being vulnerable about our areas of weakness is an act of strength that drives away shame and leads to freedom.

6. One of the signs that a culture is healthy is that people freely confess their areas of struggle to one another, confident that they are surrounded by allies who will champion their breakthrough.

7. Protecting connection is always the healthiest motivator for powerful communication.

8. We use a six-step model for healthy confrontation:

   a. Take it to the Lord.

   b. Gain perspective.

   c. Confront fear.

   d. Choose curiosity.

   e. Practice vulnerability.

   f. Learn from the experience.

8

PROTECTING A POWERFUL CULTURE

In the few years before and after our leadership transition, our church lost almost all of our volunteer force. Staff members exhausted themselves getting enough people to cover even the most basic responsibilities and we became accustomed to putting out appeal after appeal for more help. When people signaled that they were willing to volunteer, we were so desperate for help that we happily used anyone who was willing.

Slowly, as our church gained health and momentum, volunteers began to return. They were not only willing to cover needed vacancies, they were also coming with fresh ideas that would expand our ministries or launch new ones. We were, of course, thrilled by this development. However, we quickly discovered that we needed a plan for onboarding and empowering these people in a way that protected the culture we were building.

There was one particular case that forced the issue for me. A young woman came to us with a vision and a passion for starting a new ministry. She was very gifted and bold, quick to pray for people wherever she went, and it seemed like miracles just followed her. With such an obvious gifting, I was so excited that she wanted to be a part of what we were building. I quickly offered her a leadership role on the team that could work as a stepping stone to heading up this new ministry. However, I didn't take enough time to find out more about her or observe how well she worked with others.

It didn't take long before problems started to appear. This woman criticized or corrected other team members publicly and was generally negative when she spoke about our church. Though inexperienced as a leader, she had strong opinions about how everything should be done, including the areas over which she had no influence or authority. Her forceful personality overwhelmed many of our staff, and I noticed that they became subdued whenever she was around. As many people respected the obvious gifting she carried, they allowed her words to have weight, which then resulted in hurt and discouragement.

After observing her impact on the team, I asked to speak with her. I presented her with my observations and asked questions to discover if she was aware of the effect she was having on people. I let her know how I needed her to adjust if she wanted to remain in her role and stay on track for leading the new ministry down the road. I explained that we really needed to see that she could serve the team and the church with the same attitude and approach as the rest of the team.

Her response was disconcerting. "I am not willing to serve," she told me. "I will only be a part of this if I am the leader. If I am the leader, I need to be able to do it my way. I don't want you trying to change what I do just because someone might get upset."

In that moment, I realized I had been unwise in trusting her with a leadership role when this attitude was lurking under the surface and most likely could have been discovered earlier. After taking some time to process my response, I called her into another meeting and let her know that because she was unwilling to adjust, I could not entrust her with more leadership in the future. She was very disappointed and decided to remove herself from the team completely.

Walking through that experience was uncomfortable, but the silver lining was the way it revealed to us our immediate need to create a system of protection around the culture we had worked so hard to create. We had something of value—an environment full of trust, safety, healthy feedback, and strong relational connections—that was resulting in life and growth. Every week, our team had testimonies of what God was doing and was energized and excited when we came together. I could put all of that at risk if I brought people onto the team without considering how they would support and carry our relational core values. It was essential that I did not allow fear or anxiety to be reintroduced to the environment. Our tradition of bringing people in because we needed help or because they were gifted needed to change.

In order to set up a system of protection around our culture while being intentional about growth, we have purposed to do three things:

1. Train core values.
2. Hire according to core values.
3. Invest in people development.

TRAINING CORE VALUES

We decided to invite the leadership consultant who had helped us identify and develop the language of the six core values of our church to come train our staff on these values. The first step of the training was to measure how strongly we held and practiced these values. Measurement involved an anonymous survey of our full team to determine how well each person identified with the values, to what level they thought they personally displayed the value, and to what level they experienced the value within our church.

The survey results were very telling. While everyone clearly believed in the values, there were some inconsistencies between our beliefs and our behavior. We came out very strong in the areas where we had been investing, such as wholeness and healthy relationships, but tested weaker in other areas that had not been as prevalent during the season of rebuilding. It showed us where we needed to focus attention to cause our behavior to align with our beliefs, as well as gave us a starting point of comparison to continue to evaluate against in the future.

The next part of the training involved going through the values as a team to identify what each behavior would look like, how we could intentionally cultivate each value, both individually and corporately, and how we could hold one another accountable to our values. This process brought an invaluable level of clarity, ownership, and alignment around our values, and generated information we needed to adjust and strengthen every process in our organization so that it expressed, supported, and protected our values.

We adjusted every employee-related process, including hiring procedures, performance management, and criteria for promotion, to include measurements around our values. This established a clear and consistent expectation that staff members would demonstrate and promote the values, and added a purposeful feedback cycle. We knew that as the staff team carried the values, they would in turn create value expectations for their volunteer teams, which would grow the culture for the whole church. It also gave staff members the opportunity to identify areas where they needed to grow, and allowed us to allocate coaching and training resources to any place where they needed help to overcome gaps between their value system and their behavior.

The time invested in training and ongoing discussion caused the values to be adopted into the language and expectations of the team, and gave them permission to confront any time they experienced something on staff that was inconsistent with the values. I still remember the day, soon after completing the values training process with our staff, that one of our staff members walked into the front office and overheard three team members talking negatively about one of the volunteers. She immediately confronted the behavior as a violation of our value for healthy relationship. I celebrated the moment as a pivotal shift from the leadership team establishing values to the staff embracing them and boldly protecting the culture.

HIRING ACCORDING TO VALUES

In 1 Timothy 5:22, the apostle Paul instructs his protégé, Timothy, "Do not lay hands on anyone hastily" (NKJV). Laying hands on someone refers to ordination or appointment to leadership within the church. Paul is teaching Timothy to allow the character of a person to be proven before they are recognized with a position. It is wisdom to take time to evaluate not only a person's abilities, but their character as they serve and their skills in relating with others.

Along with the lesson I learned from empowering the wrong person to lead in a volunteer role, I have also learned the hard way about the cost of hiring members of staff too quickly out of anxiety to fill a role. No matter the role, adding people to the team means bringing them into our relational culture. The goal, as we grow, must always be to add people to the team who will protect and promote the values that we have already established. As we have seen firsthand, a person who does not demonstrate a commitment to our values will begin to try to shape the culture according to their personal values and belief system.

The most obvious place where a difference in values has manifested itself has been in our weekly staff meetings. These meetings have become one of the most important places for us to practice and build our team culture. We use the time to share testimonies, support and equip the team, work on exercises designed to build trust and healthy connection, and give team members a safe place to practice new skills. Staff members really enjoy and value these meetings. Some even go so far as to make sure it is recorded if they have to miss it.

However, when we have brought in new team members who didn't carry our culture, they had little value for staff meetings when they didn't live up to their expectations, especially when we did things they deemed less "spiritual." Sometimes they would get frustrated and attempt to shift the meeting towards things like evangelism, prophetic ministry, or intercession, often by making a passive-aggressive comment such as, "Why are we wasting time in here when there is a world out there that is dying?" But most often, they would make their preferences known by participating in the things they had value for, such as worship and prayer times, but visibly disconnecting during times of equipping or sharing—sitting slightly back from the group, even shutting down and getting on their phone. It was amazing to watch how having even one person disconnected in this way, especially while others were sharing vulnerably, affected the atmosphere of the entire room.

After learning that it often takes more time to let go of the wrong person than it does to hire the right person, we have now built into our recruitment process criteria that require us to look first for the demonstration of our values in potential hires. While it is important that people have the appropriate skill and gifts to do the job they are hired to do, we will hire values over skill. Skills can be taught, while values are an established and demonstrated part of a person's character. We certainly look for people who have the gifting and calling that match the role. But first, we look for people who are already serving and have built trust with the leader under whom they serve. We look for people who have demonstrated vulnerability, have made themselves available for feedback, and have the potential to be developed further. We also look for people with humility, who recognize that it is a privilege to be a part of the team and are coming to serve a greater vision than their own.

Recently, we had a part-time position open in one of our children's ministry departments. Someone came to apply for the job who looked the most qualified on paper. They had been to ministry school and had previous experience in a paid position leading a similar ministry. They had all the skills needed to do the job. However, they had not yet served anywhere in our church, which would have allowed us to evaluate how they fit with our values or worked with a team.

Alternatively, I had someone apply who was already serving in a different church department and had grown in leadership and responsibility to the point where they were greatly trusted. While they had not had schooling or previous experience in this particular ministry, they had demonstrated consistently that they carried our values and their ability to grow rapidly. We hired the person who had already been serving, knowing we could help them develop the skills they needed. It was more important to us that we could trust them to partner with and protect the culture we were building. It so happens that this person has gone on to do an amazing job and has grown the ministry. Meanwhile, the other applicant has volunteered in various ways for the church, but working with them has been challenging because they have yet to demonstrate a strong alignment with our values.

While we hire according to our values, we will also fire based on those values. I have heard it said that many organizations "hire too quickly and fire too slowly." While we have a commitment to feedback and to investing in the growth of our employees, if they will not demonstrate our values and refuse to adjust through the feedback process, we will let them go from our team. Improving our hiring process has helped to make terminations a rare occurrence, but we have let go of some employees who violated our culture repeatedly. To protect culture, every person on the team, no matter their position, must have a commitment to demonstrate and protect the values.

INVEST IN PEOPLE DEVELOPMENT

After shifting to value-based hiring and volunteer recruitment, we found that God was bringing us people who were drawn to our culture and were gifted and passionate, but didn't yet have a fully developed skill set. We were releasing these people into ministry, giving them leadership responsibility, and then finding ourselves surprised when they were floundering. They didn't know how to create plans to fulfill their ideas, didn't know how to recruit volunteers and build teams, and often didn't know how to make financial decisions and manage a budget. Our leaders were getting burned out trying to succeed and we were getting frustrated watching them struggle. We were failing them by letting them run with too much freedom and responsibility without evaluating what they needed for success and walking with them in the process of building.

There was one particular experience that made it abundantly clear that I needed to do something to remedy the strain and inefficiencies that our leaders were dealing with. We decided to partner with some new, young leaders in putting on an event to launch a new church initiative. Many things went wrong in the planning process, and our staff had to invest a lot of unscheduled time and energy to rescue the event from certain failure. After we had navigated the event successfully, I had a lot of frustrated people on my hands—both the new leaders who had been overtaken in the process, and the staff who were now exhausted.

My kneejerk reaction to the mess was simply to say, "Never again," and avoid extending that kind of responsibility to untested leaders in the future. However, I knew that wasn't a long-term solution. I decided to set up a time to debrief about the event with Tony.

After listening to the saga of everything that had gone wrong, and my suggestion that we should avoid putting young leaders in similar positions in future, Tony asked me, "So, is your main purpose to build a ministry, or is it to build people?"

"Well, when you put it like that . . . it's to build people," I answered. "If we build the people, then the ministry will happen."

"So, if you are called to build people, do you think God will send you people to develop? Or will He send you people who are ready to go?"

"People to develop," I sighed.

"And are you more concerned about protecting the church from failure, or about whether your people are developing?" he pushed.

"I have probably been trying to protect us from failure."

"So, do you think your people feel free to dream and risk new things, even if it means they fail?"

"Probably not. If we step in and take over whenever we see that something might fail, we are probably sending the message that it is not okay to make mistakes."

"That's right," Tony replied. "It sounds like it is time to create a development process to help people to succeed without leadership having to do it for them. Which means you have to change your mindset towards helping people to develop into their destiny over protecting your organization from failure. Sometimes failure is good. When you learn from failure, you grow, often faster than if you succeed at everything, every time."

Following this conversation, we began working actively toward creating a pathway that purposefully moved people through developing the skills they needed to be successful. As we began to invest in our leaders, we discovered three key components that added strength:

1. Evaluate strengths and weaknesses.
2. Encourage risk-taking.
3. Walk together.

EVALUATE STRENGTHS AND WEAKNESSES

When we add someone to our team, one of the first things we do is have them take a series of assessments to learn more about how they are wired (Myers-Briggs), their strengths and weaknesses (Strengthsfinder), and their relational style in working with others (DISC). These assessments quickly encourage self-awareness and destroy any expectation that they come as a complete leader, helping them to understand that they need—and we expect them to have—a growth mentality. Often when people start out in leadership, they come with the belief that they are expected to be fully competent in every area, which prevents them from pursuing growth or asking for help when they need it. We send them the message that weakness is not incompetence, and it is maturity that allows a person to admit their limitations and rely on the team around them. As we help people discover areas of strength where they will naturally flourish, we also let them discover areas where they will need help. This allows us to get the right people around them from the start so they learn to test ideas, ask for counsel, and work with people who are different than they are.

We are careful to lead by example in this area. For example, most of my strengths lie in my ability to influence others and to build strong relational connections. I am weaker at strategic thinking and my biggest weakness is in executing. I struggle with consistency and follow-through on repetitive tasks. While my strengths will energize, direct, and connect the team, my weaknesses mean that I am prone to making decisions too quickly without fully thinking through the future ramifications. They also mean that I may start something enthusiastically but lose interest before it is completed and shift my attention to something else.

As I have grown in understanding my strengths and weaknesses, I have purposely put people around me who are strategic thinkers and have executing strengths. When I am making decisions or developing plans, I will process with people who are strong strategically who will see things that I won't naturally see. I give them permission to dream, ask me questions, and test my ideas. I have delegated many of my repetitive tasks to people with execution strengths. For the tasks left on my list, I have empowered our administrator to set up checkpoints and reminders to ensure that I follow through on the things that I have committed to. Understanding my weaknesses causes me to lean on the strengths of the team around me, which draws out the best in all of us.

Along with helping each team member develop individual strategies like mine to leverage their strengths and weaknesses, we have also put our knowledge about one another to work in our team dynamics. For example, recently our team worked through a series of discussions and activations based around concepts from *The Five Dysfunctions of Team*. For one of the exercises, which was focused on building trust by practicing vulnerability, I had everyone on the team share their Myers-Briggs personality profile. In the process, we discovered that fifteen out of eighteen people in the room were Feelers. We only had three Thinkers! It was an important discovery for the dynamics of our team. We realized that we needed to make sure we listened to our Thinkers in decision-making processes so that we weren't always just making feeling-based decisions supported by the majority!

ENCOURAGE RISK-TAKING

Often as leaders, our instinct is to protect our people from struggle and failure. Most of us believe that failure is bad and is to be avoided at all costs. We don't believe failure could be from God. However, most people learn more through failure than they ever do through success. It is likely that the path to development for both ourselves and the people around us is to grow through adversity, risk-taking, and sometimes, through failure. If we constantly move to protect our people from challenging situations, we insulate them from the seasons they need for their growth. We must position ourselves to walk with them while overcoming the instinct to do it for them.

To develop people and help them grow, we must encourage them in risk-taking and require them to make decisions for themselves rather than giving all the answers. For example, I recently had this conversation with a new team member who was unused to making the kind of decisions I expected her to make in her role, which included event planning:

"Carla, what do you think, should we set up tables or should we sit theater-style?"

"I think that is a decision you can make," I replied.

"How about dinner—should we all eat together, or should we let people do their own thing?"

"I think you have everything in you that you need to make that decision. I think that either way, you are not going to fail. I will support you in whatever you decide, but I won't help you grow if I tell you what to do."

In all our ministries, we have introduced the challenge to innovate, experiment, and then evaluate. Failure is normal and expected as part of the experimenting process. In fact, John Maxwell, leadership author and expert, says, "If at first you do succeed, then try something harder. The willingness to take greater risks is a major key to achieving success."[1] The only requirement is that we learn something through the process. If we remove the fear of failure from people and embrace it as a normal part of growth, we will set them free to be creative, which will allow them to discover what they are truly capable of.

WALK TOGETHER

As leaders, we don't create a safe place for our people to risk unless we demonstrate that we will be there to help, support, and encourage them through the whole process. In the innovation stage, this means encouraging them to dream and explore the things God has put in their hearts to do. One of the skills I have personally sought to master over the last few years is the art of discovering what is inside people's hearts. What do they dream of doing? What do their unique set of skills, gifts, and life experiences point towards?

For example, in a one-to-one meeting with one of my team members a while back, I asked him, "So, if you have permission to dream, where do you see this role going and what do you see yourself doing?"

"I know it looks nothing like what I am doing now, but I dream about youth and young adults. I see myself working in that area one day," he replied.

"I could see that too!" I agreed. "You seem to have a natural connection to people that age. What kind of skills do you think you would need to work in that area?"

"That's a great question," he said, considering. "I've actually never thought about that. Can I have some time to think that through?"

"Sure. Let's follow up this conversation next week. I would love to

---

[1]John Maxwell, "If at first you do succeed, try something harder." May 4, 2010, John Maxwell on Leadership Blog johnmaxwell.com/blog/if-at-first-you-do-succeed-try-something-harder

help resource you if you identify some skills you need to develop."

This is how we get the ball rolling with innovation—we want people to innovate in their areas of passion. Through asking good questions, we guide people through the process of self-discovery and generating powerful solutions. From there, we move into the experiment stage, where we stay current with their decision-making process and provide the support they need to grow and execute their ideas. We stretch them by giving them opportunities for practice in places where making mistakes doesn't feel like a public failure. Staff meetings and smaller gathering become incubators where people have the opportunity to try things they haven't done before in a safe environment. In this way, we position ourselves to champion their destiny while pushing them to grow towards it. People will allow you to stretch them if they know you care for them, and they will take risks if they know they are not standing alone.

Soon after my initial conversation with the team member who expressed interest in youth ministry, he began working with our youth as a volunteer. He threw himself in with a goal of strongly supporting the youth leaders, and started training himself with leadership resources from Danny's online school, The Life Academy, as well as others we offered him. He faithfully used every opportunity we gave him to develop his skills—preaching, pastoring, confrontation, and working with parents—and in the process, built trust with everyone around him. When the leaders of the ministry recently came to me to let me know they felt it was time to step down, they strongly recommended him as their successor. I was able to offer him the position as leader of our youth ministry! This is the payoff we love to see in supporting our people as they risk and run after what God has put in their hearts.

Lastly, in the evaluation stage, we walk with people by helping them manage and learn from the fallout of failure, as well as celebrating their success. As we are learning to celebrate one another, it has been fun at team gatherings to watch team members begin to "tell on" one another when someone has tried something new or done something well. Often, it has the effect of inviting more feedback from others on the team about how they have noticed that person has been growing, how they have personally been impacted by that person, and how proud we are of them. I have purposed to write cards and give surprise gifts, not just to celebrate the results we want to see, but also to celebrate the risks being taken and even the failures that have happened on the pathway to success.

CONCLUSION

Though it's only been a few years since we adopted our policies of training and hiring by core values and investing in people, we have seen so much growth and acceleration as an organization that we have decided to build our leadership team fully on a servant-based leadership model. Now, our primary goal as senior leaders is to identify current and potential leaders who carry our values and have a vision for ministry, invest in their growth and development, and give them the help and resources they need to be successful. We believe that if we invest ourselves in identifying and developing champions, those champions in turn will invest in building the church, our church family will be mobilized, and our community and state will be impacted as a result. Building champions is our strategy to see our corporate vision and mission fulfilled.

SUMMARY

1. We protect a powerful culture of honor and connection in three ways:
    a. We train our people in our core values.
    b. We hire according to our core values.
    c. We invest in developing people.

1. Our three primary strategies for developing people are:

    a. We evaluate strengths and weaknesses so we can leverage them effectively, both for individual growth and effectiveness in team collaboration.

    b. We encourage risk-taking by requiring decision-making and lowering fear of failure.

    c. We walk with people in the developmental process by supporting them as they innovate around their dreams and calling, experiment and build new skills, and evaluate and learn from results, both positive and negative.

EPILOGUE

BUILDING MOMENTUM IN A CULTURE OF HONOR

Recently, a new employee came into my office and asked if he could read me something he had written the previous evening after work. He explained that he had been reflecting on the impact that working at Northgate was having on his heart, and had been moved to put it into words. He pulled out a note and began, becoming visibly moved by what he was sharing with me as he spoke.

"There is an amazing freedom I feel amongst the staff," he read. "A freedom that allows my dysfunction to come out into the open, and yet I feel completely loved. This love actually compels me to run hard to God for health and growth and healing. I can see my weakness, and yet I have become so convinced of my true calling and identity that I no longer feel the disdain for myself that I once believed I would live with forever."

This note was especially significant to me, because this employee had not been with us through the season of dramatic change or the stages of establishing and training in core values. He was describing something real that was happening simply through the *experience* of working in our culture and being around the people on our team. As he experienced a true culture of honor, it was a natural process for him to grow in self-awareness, begin to pursue wholeness and healing without shame, and to experience freedom as a result. That is the fruit of a culture of honor.

Over time, I have heard many leaders in different settings declare, "We desire to have a culture of honor." Yet as I have looked around these settings and noticed the anxiety and disconnection in the atmosphere, the lack of honest feedback flowing to and from the leader, and the burnout or constant turnover of leaders and staff members, I have come to recognize that statement often means, "I want everyone to honor me." The idea of honor has been misused many times by powerless, fearful leaders as an excuse to demand respect and apply religious pressure to control those around them.

A true culture of honor is others-focused instead of self-serving, and first begins in the heart of the leader. We can only reproduce around us what we have cultivated within us. The pathway to becoming a powerful, honoring leader begins with a commitment to self-awareness. We must learn what is present inside our hearts, how it is shaping our behavior, and therefore, how we are affecting everyone around us. When we have the courage to pursue truth and healing, we begin to discover places where fear has dominated our hearts and influenced our relational behaviors. Often, we have layers of fear that have gained access to our hearts through the experience of past relational pain and suffering. This fear has shaped the way that we view the world and react to circumstances. When we see through the lens of fear, other people are perceived as a threat and we move to protect ourselves from them at all costs. While fear remains, it hinders our ability to build powerful, healthy, and life-giving connections, as love cannot grow where fear is present.

As you may have noticed, fear showed up again and again in my journey of learning to lead. I did not realize how much I had learned to live afraid until I walked through many difficult situations that revealed my instinctive reaction to run and hide out of a strong urge to self-protect. In others, I have seen the same fear drive them to aggressively fight those they care about. Overcoming fear and the lies that have fed it has been the subject of many coaching appointments and Sozo sessions. As I have gained increasing freedom, I have learned the importance of fear-resilience—the ability to identify fear as soon as it rises in my heart and confront it before it overwhelms my emotions and controls my behavior. It has been a long, at-times frustrating, and yet intentional journey.

Yet the more we overcome fear, the more we gain the ability to pick up and use the tools and skills necessary first to be a powerful person who builds healthy, connected relationships, and then to be a powerful leader who creates an environment where others get to grow in the same journey. It is a trained skill to learn to see people through the lens of honor rather than the lens of fear, and refuse to turn honor off, even when their behavior scares us. As we honor people by seeing them as God sees them, we learn to protect our relational connections through practicing healthy confrontation and creating a safe place for people to give us feedback.

As with our new employee, when people come in and experience a culture where others believe the best about them, even when their weakness is on display, and take the risk to speak the truth to them, they in turn will gain the courage to come out of hiding and confront their own fears. A true encounter with this kind of selfless love drives fear away. With fear gone, people come alive, become willing to dream and risk, and results begin to multiply.

While the primary focus of our leadership team has been on building culture, the resulting unity in our team has attracted other exciting results. Our church has grown, our finances have increased, and the number of salvations, miraculous healings, and testimonies of transformation have multiplied. Our church is unrecognizable from the moment of crisis we were in when I walked into Dennis's office four years ago! We have not only gone from surviving to thriving—we are actively laying a foundation to impact generations to come.

My desire in writing this book is to see thousands of people developed to lead with the heart of heaven in their families, churches, schools, and workplaces—even before they have an official position of leadership. The call to become powerful leaders who build powerful, healthy relational cultures is not for the special few. It is for every one of us who has become a son or daughter of a the most powerful, relational Person in the universe. We are all called to look like our Father and carry His fearless love to the world. May we all rise with fresh passion to answer this call in the days ahead.

ACKNOWLEDGMENTS

Aaron—I love you. You have been my biggest champion and partner in the journey of discovery. Thank you for believing in me more than I believed in myself!

Ashton and Ava—I love how excited you have been for Mom to write a book, long before you will understand what it is about! May it somehow be a part of creating your legacy. I love you!

Northgate staff and leadership team—Thank you for having the courage and vulnerability to go on this journey of transformation. It has been a delight to risk, fail, learn, and grow together. I am proud of us!